DEATHMAN PASS ME BY:
Two Years on Death Row

Borgo Bioviews No. 3
ISSN 0743-9628

DEATHMAN PASS ME BY

TWO YEARS ON DEATH ROW
PHILIP BRASFIELD with JEFFREY M. ELLIOT

BORGO BIOVIEWS #3 ISSN 0743-9628

BORGO PRESS / WILDSIDE PRESS

www.wildsidepress.com

To My Mother and Father—
For their love invested
in me that overflowed . . . .

How sweetly did they float upon the wings
of silence, through the empty-vaulted night
at every fall smoothing the raven-down
of darkness 'til it smiled. —John Milton

Library of Congress Cataloging in Publication Data:

Brasfield, Philip, 1949-
  Deathman pass me by.

  (Borgo bioviews ; no. 3)
  1. Brasfield, Philip, 1949-   . 2. Prisoners—Texas—biography.
3. Death row—Texas. I. Elliot, Jeffrey M. II. Title. III. Series.
HV9475.T4B7   364.1'523'0924 [B]   82-4126
ISBN 0-89370-164-5   AACR2
ISBN 0-89370-264-1

Produced, designed, and published by R. Reginald and Mary A. Bur-
gess, The Borgo Press, P.O. Box 2845, San Bernardino, CA 92406,
USA. Cover and title page design by Michael Pastucha. Photographs
of Philip Brasfield and family by Doug Magee.

CONTENTS

PHOTOGRAPHS

ACKNOWLEDGEMENTS

There isn't enough space to thank everyone who has ever encouraged me to write. So, instead of attempting the impossible, I'll just say thanks to whose who planted good seeds in fertile soil, and then had the patience to watch the plants sprout and slowly grow.

I would be remiss, however, if I did not thank my collaborator, Dr. Jeffrey M. Elliot, who gave generously of his time and advice, and who provided a helpful critique of the manuscript. Jeff and his assistant, Anne Fishman, painstakingly went over the manuscript, page by page and line by line, making numerous suggestions and criticisms that had a significant impact on the final form of this book.

Finally, to my brothers and sisters in prison and on death row, again, space doesn't permit me to share much of our struggle with the folks at home. Maybe my next book can do that. I am grateful to each of you, however, for your brave stance in the struggle. We *shall* overcome!

Philip Brasfield

Tennessee Colony, Texas
October, 1982

ONE

I'm not a criminal. I'm not a kidnapper and not a child killer. Some people believe me to be, though, and they believe this so strongly that I've been tried, convicted, and sentenced to death.

On March 17, 1978, as I stood in the Wichita County, Texas, Courthouse, feeling the eyes of the spectators behind me, I waited tensely for the verdict.

"Guilty!" The power of that word was a blow that would send me reeling for months. I was reminded of the utter helplessness and abject terror that I'd experienced only four years earlier during the split seconds before my car was struck by a massive freight train. But this time, the vehicle of death was the implacable force of the law.

After I heard the pronouncement, I looked up at the jury box. Not one person would meet my glance. Each head was bowed as if in meditation; their eyes could have bored holes into the floor. All I heard was Judge William Shaver shuffling some papers; someone behind me scraped a chair on his way out. The burly deputies who were assigned as guards motioned me through the side door, where I joined my ashen-faced mother and my wife, who was in tears.

Mark Hall, one of my two court-appointed attorneys from Lubbock, Texas, stepped into the room to reassure us. Mark said he didn't think the jury would be able to bring back the death sentence during the punishment phase of my trial. But he was visibly shaken and seemed more in need of comfort than we. After a few more words, he slipped out of the room and left us alone.

Capital murder statutes differ from state to state. In Texas, a capital murder trial is conducted in two parts, and called a "bifurcated trial." In the first phase of the trial, a defendant's guilt or innocence is determined by evidence produced in open court. There is only a second phase if the defendant is found guilty. In this portion, the jury hears testimony and must answer affirmatively to two questions posed by Texas statutes: Article 37.071 (a) requires the jury in a capital murder case to decide whether the conduct of the defendant who caused the

7

death of the victim was commited deliberately, and with the reasonable expectation that the death of the deceased would result. If the jury believes the defendant's conduct was deliberate and death of the victim was expected, it then casts an affirmative vote and considers the next question. Article 37.071 (b) requires the jury to decide whether there is a probability that the defendant would commit criminal acts of violence that would constitute a continuing threat to society. The jury comes to this decision by reviewing the defendant's past criminal record, character evidence, psychiatric testimony, or extraneous matters. If the jury answers the above two questions affirmatively, it can vote for death under the law and the judge of the court must, by law, sentence the defendant to death.

I looked into my mother's eyes and saw her pain. I put my arm around her and Josie, my wife, and as I drew them close to me, I quoted a phrase from the Bible that had given me courage: "For I am persuaded that neither death, nor life, nor angels, nor principalities, nor power of things to come, nor height, nor depth, nor any other creature, shall be able to separate us from the love of God which is in Jesus Christ our Lord" (Romans 8: 38-39). That was all I could say, and it was all that needed saying, because I felt each of them start to relax.

My mother asked if I thought the jury would answer the two questions in the affirmative during the punishment phase of the trial, which would force the judge to sentence me to death. I told her, as I had before, that I didn't believe there was any evidence against me. "How in God's name could they find you guilty then, Phil?" she asked. "Mama, I don't know. We've just got a little time together so let's try not to worry," I said, trying to comfort her.

She asked if I'd like some coffee, and then left Josie and I sitting quietly together; the minutes passed too quickly. I told Josie that if the unthinkable happened and the jury returned with affirmative answers to both questions, I didn't want Ma to hear the judge sentence me to die. Josie agreed. She didn't think Ma could stand it, especially considering my father's recent death and the toll my trial had already taken.

I'd served sixty-six days in the Lubbock County Jail when my father had died at our family home in Slaton, Texas. At first I just couldn't believe it. Only a few days earlier my parents and Josie had visited me. The jailer had been kind and had allowed Papa to come up and talk to me through the bars so that we could grasp hands. Although my father had been ill for several years, his death shocked me, and with his passing, a part of me died too.

Papa had worked for the Santa Fe Railroad, beginning as a fireman on the old steam engines. During his thirty-five years of service, he worked his way up to the position of division engineer, having the most seniority over the other engineers in that division of the Santa Fe. Papa was the hardest working man I've ever known. It wasn't uncommon for him to work twelve or fourteen hours and then come home and work around the house or in the garden until he was exhausted. The long night hours on the train, the long hours working at home in the daytime, and the alcohol he drank to keep going, took their toll and left him living out his final years in a shell of a once fine body. He developed emphysema, then congestive heart failure, and later painful osteoarthritis. The strain and anger caused by my arrest was just too much for him.

The authorities in the Lubbock County Jail wouldn't let me attend the funeral, but, after pleading with the judge, I was finally taken to the funeral home to see Papa for the last time. My whole family was there, and that was the last time all of us would be together. They each rushed to the back door of Englund's Funeral Home and hugged and kissed me. My sister, Nell, and her children were gathered around me, as was Susan English, my first wife, and our daughters, Stephanie and Amber. Josie was there too, along with Mickey Swinburn, who had been married to Nell for a number of years. This sad get-together with my family and relations was the last time I remember feeling secure and loved without question. It was the last time my little girls would be able to touch their Daddy—and even at that I couldn't return their embrace, because I was shackled by handcuffs.

The scene remains etched in my mind, all of us sitting together in a small anteroom, with my father's body lying peacefully there just beyond us. I could feel Papa's presence and finally understood his last words to me: "Be strong!" I had no choice; to do otherwise would permanently shatter our family.

The deputy opened the door and told me I was wanted back inside the courtroom: it was time for sentencing. I quickly finished my coffee and put out my cigarette.

I told Ma that I'd rather she stay in the side-room, and she reluctantly agreed. I thus believed that both she and Josie would be spared the district attorney's anticipated scathing attack. I never noticed that Josie had slipped into the courtroom after I was seated.

Dennis McGill, my other court-appointed attorney, leaned over the counsel table and suggested that I try to stay calm and not show any emotion, regardless of what the D.A., Alton Griffin, might say. I told Dennis that I was doing okay and not to worry. Just then, I heard my wife's familiar cough and turned to see her sitting about eight feet behind me. She mouthed, "I love you," as the judge came in and sat down.

       *   *   *   *   *   *

I was born in Slaton, Texas on August 31, 1949, to June and Paul Brasfield. I'm their second child, an only son. My sister, Nell, was born in 1936, also in Slaton. My mother lost two other children in pregnancy. Slaton is a small, wind-swept farming community located sixteen miles southeast of Lubbock, in an area of Texas called the South Plains.

I attended St. Joseph's Catholic School in the parish where we went to church. My early childhood memories are filled with scenes of the beautiful, richly-orange California poppies that grew profusely in Mama's backyard. I'd go out into the heat of summer and lay among the poppies, watching the bees busily collecting pollen.

Summer was always my favorite season; during the fall and winter months I was plagued with bronchial asthma, and in the spring, my allergies would replace the wheezing and coughing. After starting first grade, I was removed from school and hospitalized. It was impossible to play with other children, so I spent much of my time reading or playing the piano.

Between railroad trips, my father and mother rebuilt most of our family home. They were a working team. During those years, Papa didn't seem to have much time for me. But I do remember when we'd all pile into the Pontiac and drive to New Mexico to spend a few days with friends who owned land there. Sleeping in the primitive log cabins, cooking on woodstoves, eating by kerosene lamplight after fishing for sparkling rainbow trout, these were the highlights of those glorious summers. Nell and I could ride the gentle horses all day for a dollar. Those trips influenced me for life. My favorite kind of country is still up in the mountains, where the air is fresh from the alpine heights and the verdant pine trees. My memories sustained me even on death row.

In 1956, two events had a monumental effect on me. First, on a warm spring day while visiting my paternal grandfather, I saw him suddenly die. Like all young people, I was troubled by the thought of death and confused by the notion of "going to sleep forever." Death didn't frighten me, but I was sad to lose Papaw. There was a feeling of loss and loneliness I'd never experienced before. I'd go into his bedroom and run my damp fingers over his hairbrush and other personal effects lying on his dresser. In the old chiffarobe I'd take deep breaths of that smell so human that hangs onto our clothes even after we die. I wondered if his spirit had stayed in Mamaw's house or if it had travelled instantly across time and space to join our ancestors in Tennessee.

Later that year, on August 24th, my sister gave birth to her oldest daughter, Jo Claire. Nell and Mama had spent months talking to the child's father, trying to convince him to do the "honorable" thing: to marry my sister. Not surprisingly, he didn't want to be "tied down" and remained opposed to marriage.

My parents' feelings were obvious and I've always been grateful for their candor. I was told the truth about sex and procreation and was never confused about it. Even more apparent was the example of responsibility they provided (and my sister reinforced) by giving birth to Claire, when many other alternatives were possible.

There were repercussions, however, that I didn't comprehend at first. My sister's friends drifted away, and worse, there were some people in town who reacted with anger and hostility. St. Joseph's was no exception—I received support from our priest, but very little from the nuns and children. I enjoyed my duties as an altar boy, but at first didn't like the days of schoolwork. Later my grades improved, as did my self-image. Gradually, the taunts directed at my physical limitations didn't matter.

Two years after Claire was born, my sister married a local boy. They moved in and out of our lives whenever one of her husband's "get-rich-quick" schemes failed, or when Nell and her children became the victims of his violent temper. He'd act like a madman, then suddenly calm down, and be on his best behavior for months. Inevitably, however, another violent incident would occur.

Nell's husband was the first to introduce me to horses, thereby changing my life. After we acquired the first few, I spent most of my spare time with the stock, and became an accomplished rider and horseman. Eventually, we acquired over a dozen head of horses.

On November 22, 1963, the nation wept for President John F. Kennedy. School was dismissed early and I went home and watched as the president's body was buried, and as his accused assassin was murdered. Perhaps it was my age, or my idealism, or maybe both; whatever the reason, I pinpoint those tragic events as a major catalyst in my life. Afterwards, I began questioning everything, and stopped believing in many of the political and patriotic maxims we all learn in grammar school. The only political figure I had ever really loved was gone.

TWO

The influence of one's peers during adolescence is a powerful force. To resist it can result in ostracism, but to join the crowd can compromise one's unique character.

In Slaton High School, playing football is the most acceptable thing a young man can do. Not playing football may not be the *least* acceptable thing, but it comes close. I didn't play sports in high school, but joined the school band. Secretly, there was always a feeling of having the best of both worlds, since after a game, no matter who won or lost, band members were winners. Band members were never carried away with injuries, and didn't have to endure the grueling regimen of training.

Despite an outward appearance of self-assurance, I remained quite shy in high school, and didn't take part in the adolescent social climbing of a small town. My grades through high school were average, although I failed English. My membership in the band ended after some of us were caught drinking and admitted our guilt.

By long-established custom, booze was smuggled aboard the band bus on the long road trips from the football games. The night we were caught, a fellow carouser became ill and vomited into his helmet. The contents were dumped out of an open window and landed on the window of the school superintendent's car, almost causing the poor fellow to careen off the road. The jig, as they say, was up. The price of our honesty, when confronted with the evidence, was expulsion from the band with which I loved to play. I felt it was unfair for the administration to allow only the honest members to bear the brunt of the punishment. I lost the credits needed for graduation.

I dated selectively in those years, and had only one serious romance before quitting high school to work on the Santa Fe Railroad. The girl I was dating at the time was honest enough to tell me she thought I had a drinking problem. I'd thought about that possibility myself, but had invented all sorts of excuses. My father always drank openly around the family, and our friends drank, so I thought nothing of the nights I'd over-indulge and come home crocked. People generally aren't ashamed of being drunk, since so many jokes are exchanged about "the night before." It's only when drinking becomes a real problem that it's a source of discomfort and eventually considered to be a social stigma.

I worked in several railroad depots, learning Morse Code and how to fill out the many forms and reports for shipping and receiving boxcars of material. While stationed at the small Maryneal, Texas depot, my local draft board ordered me to report to Amarillo, Texas, for induction into the United States Army.

At the time, the war in Vietnam was being seen daily by millions of people on the evening news. In a sense, every man, woman, and child of the sixties are veterans of that war. All of us lost a part of ourselves there. I hadn't thought much about war before my draft notice came, but I thought of little else afterwards. The station agent where I worked was a patriotic veteran of World War II, and so encouraged me to join the Navy, as he had. Wanting to be in almost any other branch of the service except the Army, I drove to Sweetwater and talked to the recruiter there, took the tests, and received a date to report. I sent a notice of resignation over the company telegraph lines and gave up my position. Then I called home and asked to speak to Papa. Ma must have sensed something was wrong, because she asked if anything had happened. I told her I'd joined the Navy and would leave for the coast in a week.

I went from one party to another, bidding old friends goodbye. Several of us barbecued a goat and bought a keg of beer, and made a night of the last party I attended. When I left on the bus to report to Dallas, I believed I would not be home again until I was out of the Navy. I didn't want to go, but probably no young man ever really wants to fight in old men's wars.

I was determined to do what I could for my country. I didn't realize how quickly the naivete of west Texas isolation and immaturity would be stripped away. The rawboned Catholic kid from Slaton, Texas would never be the same.

After being sworn in, approximately eighty young men and I were housed overnight, fed a soggy breakfast, and bussed to the airport, where we flew to San Diego, California for induction. It was dark when we landed at Lindbergh Field; a sharp smell of salt hit me when I stepped off the plane, as I encountered the ocean for the first time.

A group of servicemen from different branches were standing at a boarding gate, some with aluminum crutches, their empty trouser legs blowing in the breeze. These men were leaving the service. As quickly as I could, I tossed my sweat-stained, straw cowboy hat in a garbage can. I had already been called "Tex" by some of the First and Second Class Petty Officers. I'd been the only one wearing what I always wore: boots, hat, western shirt, and Levi's.

Recruit training was about as routine as one might expect. I was made recruit master-at-arms for our company, and spent extra hours making sure the barracks was ready for morning inspections. Each day was a disappointment, because the inspectors would always manage to find something wrong. As time passed, the persistent drilling of Chief Hoyt, our Company Commander, and our hard work as a team, allowed us to march proudly with the battallion flag prominently unfurled in front of Company 455.

There were two incidents in boot camp which stand out. The day the American astronauts landed on the moon, in 1969, a friend and I smoked marijuana with a petty officer, and heard from him, first hand, about Vietnam. What few misconceptions I retained about American involvement were deflated that day; it seemed obscene to hear the base cheering the moon landing. How ironic that the technology which permitted man to be catapulted to the moon also permitted so many lives to be snuffed out in Vietnam.

The other incident was just as revealing. I'd been chosen as a member of the drum and bugle corps, and after a San Diego Chargers game one night, the corps members were invited to meet President Richard Nixon. At close range, Nixon seemed to be wearing makeup, and as I shook his cold, clammy hand, I had the unsettling but sharp impression that this was no real person, but some clever mechanical automaton. Nixon briefly talked about the "threat from the East," and then turned and faced us with a sloppy salute followed by his famous grimacing smile. He entered the huge presidential helicopter and flew away into infamy and history.

When I returned home, many of my school friends were back from boot camp too, although most were in the Army. I was scheduled for Radioman School, while their orders specified Vietnam. We spent hours talking about the resentment each of us had felt while stationed at various bases around the country. The time passed quickly and I wanted to take one last hunting trip before leaving for school and sea duty. My cousin and I travelled to Southland, Texas, and spent the day hiking up and down small arroyos and hills. That night, while cleaning an antique rifle, I accidentally shot myself through the foot. I was treated at a nearby airbase and, within a month, flew back to San Diego.

I thought that the paperwork would have explained my absence to the Naval authorities, but unfortunately I had to retell my story many times before my name was taken off the A.W.O.L. list. However, the wound in my foot had not healed; it became infected and I was admitted to Balboa Naval Hospital. The bottom of the cast had turned black with seeping blood, and my foot was suppurating and badly discolored upon examination. It was a high grade infection; later I learned it was called osteomyelitis.

The weeks passed slowly in the orthopedics ward. I was surrounded by men who had been badly wounded in Vietnam and came to know them well, as I listened to their tales of horror. We were obsessed with the topic, talking in hushed, toneless voices. Multiple amputees were housed around me; their repeated advice was, "Don't go to 'Nam.' " As I slowly recovered from the infection and shattered metaparcils in my foot, I was placed on temporary duty in the histology lab. Thousands of pap smears were done there for surrounding bases each week. Whenever a positive slide was found, the technicians would ring a small bell. The one who'd find the most positive slides would buy the beer at the end of the day.

I would go into town with my temporary liberty card and stump around on a walking cast. The hospital is just across the road from Balboa Park and the famous San Diego Zoo, where I spent many afternoons. There were anti-war rallies at the park almost every weekend, and sometimes I'd go over to the edge of the crowds and listen. What I heard made infinitely more sense than the simple-minded propaganda on television.

When I returned to Camp Nimitz after being discharged from the hospital, I learned that the Navy had filed charges against me for malingering and for willfully causing a self-inflicted injury to avoid duty. The Navy's charges were clearly spurious, but I still had to fight them. After an over-zealous Lieutenant, Junior Grade, convinced my commanding officer to give me a Captain's Mast, nothing more happened. Yet each time I requested sick call, or put in a request for liberty, I was reminded of the "pending charges."

The more I heard and read, the more I opposed American involvement in Southeast Asia. I spent much of my free time in the library on base, and attending anti-war rallies off base at night. The offices of the *San Diego Street Truckin' Authority*, a small radical paper, served as a meeting place for anti-war activists. On occasion, men were seen lurking in a parked van across the street. They would step out of the van and snap photographs of people entering or leaving the building.

On October 15, 1969, I participated in a mass demonstration. I later learned that over two million Americans had marched that day. One night, against the backdrop of a bronze sunset in an agate coastal sea, a young Vietnamese man and woman spoke to those of us gathered around a campfire at Ocean Beach. Their anguished reports of what America was doing to their country deeply touched me. From that night I was determined to follow the haunting cries of those with whom I had shared hospital bedspace. I'd refuse to go to Vietnam if so ordered, and, in fact, would refuse to participate in any capacity as a part of America's war machine. It became not only a matter of conscious determination, but of principles and ethics, too.

16

It's never easy to defy tradition. In my family, most of the males had dutifully served in times of war. But as a growing number of Americans were beginning to realize, the occupation of Vietnam and Cambodia was an immoral, self-defeating act of imperialism. After I informed the Naval authorities of my decision, I faced a court-martial and was assigned to "X-Division" with other servicemen in trouble with the Naval Command. The resisters were treated with respect by the other members of the X-Division, but were often badly treated by base security command. We hung together during the gray, wet winter of 1969 and the spring of 1970. Most of us were released en masse with less than honorable discharges, but by some stroke of fate, I received a General Discharge under honorable conditions—"for the benefit of the Navy."

During this period, my alcohol intake continued. I drank at a steady rate, although I preferred marijuana. A friend from the Navy and I took the last passenger train as far as Clovis, New Mexico. Then we rode on to Slaton with my parents. It is hard to explain just how I felt and how my values about life and my newfound respect for counter-cultures would set me apart from those I'd known so long in Texas. I was in for some difficult times, but I had seriously underestimated the reaction of the townspeople. There were unspoken rules that could not be broken. I was regarded as a coward, a traitor, and a pariah for refusing to fight. It would be years before some of these people realized they had been fooled, and that the detested "flower children" and war resisters had been right.

THREE

I joined the War Resisters League in May, 1970 and soon became a local organizer. Armed with their encouragement and printed matter, I began canvassing the town. I learned that many of the people I approached were honestly afraid to say anything against the government's policy in Southeast Asia. There were very few adults who would hear me out, and I was even told to stay out of local restaurants and watering holes I'd frequented most of my life.

Likewise, I had minimal success when I spoke to the teenagers and others who still kept alive the tradition of cruising around town. Much as I had been before joining the Navy, they remained happy, apathetic, and content enough to drink beer and listen to music and not do much else.

There was a small group, however, who not only listened but were supportive of the anti-war movement and of me. As word spread, the local police would pull up as I talked quietly, and would find reason to either tell me to move on, or take me to the police station for questioning. After speaking in Lubbock one night, I was beaten up by three locals who'd tried to anger me with verbal abuse. I was hit with an empty whiskey bottle and left near my car. I realized then that my late-night benedictions had to stop. Thereafter, my political rhetoric was reserved for the close, trusted associates with whom I travelled for added safety. During the autumn of 1970, I met the woman who would become my first wife. Susan Sander was a senior attending Wilson High School. After a stormy courtship, during which her parents forbade us to see one another, Susan and I travelled to California for a few months. We returned to Slaton and married in August, 1971. There was no honeymoon. Our memories of life in Los Angeles and of sailing to Catalina Island would have to do. Susan was pregnant and I had to go to work.

It was not all connubial bliss, though. We fought over the smallest things, and I'd handle my anger and resentment with the old standbys of alcohol and marijuana. A series of jobs and apartments, each decreasing in quality, had us moving almost every four months. When our first daughter, Stephanie Ann, was born on March 11, 1972, I began the long struggle of trying to regain control over my life, my drinking, and my battered self-respect, all now in ruins.

Through our fathers' generosity, Susan and I bought a mobile home and settled on the property where my horses had once been kept. The livestock was gone now, having been sold while I was in the Navy. We planted a huge organic garden, then later built a greenhouse. I worked as a carpenter, painter, and at other manual jobs. A brief experiment as a hairdresser ended in disaster, and, not surprisingly, more drinking.

Our second daughter, Amber Lea, was born on December 17, 1973, a little over twenty-one months after Stephanie. The temporary jobs ended in February, 1974, when I was hired by the Santa Fe Railroad for the third and last time.

I began working on the paint crew, applying industrial paint to anything (inside or out) that needed it. Susan was now working part-time at a Dairy Queen; with my wages from the railroad, we could finally see our economic future brightening. Having more money now than ever before, I began to get back some of my self-esteem. At about this time also, many Americans were beginning to recognize the insanity of the war, causing some of my neighbors to view my opinions in a different light.

After work one day, I was waiting for a train to clear the unmarked crossing near the edge of town, planning to go down to the paint-gang foreman's house. I'd stopped off at the V.F.W. Club for a few drinks with a friend, but was far from drunk. As the caboose of the train passed by, I failed to notice another train approaching the crossing from the other direction, and started across the intersection just as the engine of the second train came into view, its airhorns howling.

I jammed my foot hard against the accelerator, flooding the engine and stalling out. There were perhaps three or four seconds between the time I first saw the freight and the sound of the impact that sent my car careening madly sideways down the tracks in a shattering symphony of broken glass and twisted steel. I remember seeing the shocked faces of the train crew, sickly recognizing both the engineer and brakeman.

The car was hurled like a leaf in a hurricane. I was lifted and flung against a flattened child's carseat that padded my body as it smashed into the passenger door. The car was knocked away from the behemoth of iron. I had a horrible realization that the train was going to hit the car again.

The second impact carried the car another sixty feet down the track, derailed the lead engine and following units, and ground us to a shuddering stop. My car had sheared off a rail switch and partially aligned the tracks to another rail. I don't remember getting out of the car. To this day, I don't know how or why I escaped with my life. I seem to have the clearest memory of being suspended above the destruction and flying from the wreckage. Later examination found both car doors and windows closed tight.

The entire right side of my body was numb and I was bleeding badly from a huge cut on my forehead. Nothing seemed broken; I was rushed to the hospital by a former teacher who happened to see the wreck as he drove towards the tracks.

Our family physician hastily sutured the gaping head wound without benefit of x-rays. I was sick, dizzy, and in terrible pain all night, and, upon reexamination, was told to report to the Santa Fe Memorial Hospital in Temple, Texas, which was nearly four hundred miles away.

Ma, my wife, and the children rode with me, and the longer we were on the road, the sicker I became. I was losing the sight in my left eye and the swelling on the injured part of my head looked terrible. Later, after routine x-rays, we learned that I had sustained a very bad concussion and intracranial bleeding. There was concern that if blood clots developed and lodged in a lung or artery near the brain, the result might be fatal; but through medication and several I.V.'s, the clots dissolved. After two weeks in the hospital, I returned home and finished healing before going back to work.

On my return, I was transferred to the bridge gang, and spent the next year working from the border town of Presidio, Texas to Newton, Kansas. During that period, the crew and I worked in at least five floods, where railroad lines and bridges were washed out and had to be repaired or rebuilt. It was both fascinating and brutally hard, but it was railroading. Living conditions were very poor on the company-furnished sleeping cars. Each car was a converted mail or baggage car from the retired rolling stock of bygone passenger service days. We would roast in the summer and freeze in the winter. The stoves and water heaters ran on kerosene power. Fuel was pumped from fifty-five gallon barrels and hand-carried to the five gallon fuel tanks inside the cars. After a few days one got used to the kerosene fumes.

After a year, I took a leave of absence from the railroad to attend a training program for alcohol counseling. I had joined Alcoholics Anonymous after the train wreck and had finally rid myself of dependence on alcohol. I now wanted to know more about myself. Life had taken on more meaning after the train wreck. By attempting to relate to God as I understood Him, and by practicing the Twelve Steps of A.A., I stayed sober.

I was in my car when I heard on the radio that the last American troops had finally been withdrawn from Vietnam. Crying, I drove home slowly to hold my children, and to pray that our country would never again take part in such a pointless, violent action. The scars of the Vietnamese men, women, and children are witness to those tragic times. The wounds on the bodies and minds of American servicemen, too, bear witness to the destructiveness of mindless patriotism; many of these wounds have yet to heal long after the napalm-scorched soil has cooled.

The Alcohol and Drug Counselor Training Program (A.D.C.T.P.) at Fort Lyon, Colorado proved to be a unique experience. The eight-month program included both practical experience, classroom training, and intense sessions of group psychotherapy, coupled with classes in Transactional Analysis. A graduate of the program receives an Associate of Applied Science Degree from Otero Junior College in La Junta, Colorado, and is certified in many states to work as an alcohol and drug-counselor.

Before going to Fort Lyon, I put in two months as an intern at the Veteran's Administration Hospital in Big Spring, Texas. There I participated in its Substance Abuse Program, learning to work within the program and becoming familiar with the many forms that must be kept for the patients. I was asked to conduct alcohol education classes, rap sessions, and A.A. meetings. The interns were on twenty-four hour call for any potential crisis in the hospital ward and there was very little free time.

An intern is subjected to a great amount of pressure and is evaluated by the program's staff. Weekly progress reports are made to the director of the program, then phoned into the student coordinator at Fort Lyon. Once an intern reaches Fort Lyon, the staff there has an excellent idea of how he or she has held up under the pressure. They're also able to determine if the student is still motivated to change. Without that desire, the program cannot succeed.

We had classes in the psychology, sociology, physiology of alcoholism, ethics of counseling, first aid and detoxification training, nutrition courses, and Transactional Analysis sessions, as well as marathon group encounters. Each class consists of thirty students, but classes are staggered so that one group will be halfway through the training when a new class arrives. Except for holidays, and a yearly break for the instructors (who also hold positions on the hospital staff), there is a continuous flow of people into and out of A.D.C.T.P.

A large percentage of the students in A.D.C.T.P. are former addicts, drug abusers, or recovering alcoholics. The personal insight which is gained through the total training experience either brings about changes in an individual or frightens him away. In almost every class there are some who cannot or will not change, and they simply drop out or resume drinking or drug use, which results in their dismissal.

Fort Lyon is a psychiatric hospital. Many of the patients there are casualties of the Second World War, Korea, and, of course, Vietnam. As I'd walk down the cavernous halls, I'd get the feeling that the emotionally broken men I saw were the lasting legacies of war. Later, as I grew close to a few of them, I'd find that my feelings were well-founded.

While classroom training takes precedence over treatment, each student is also required to work shifts in various hospital wards. When I attended school there, we were responsible for keeping the library open until 11 P.M., so other students could do research, as well as work an overnight duty in one of the alcohol treatment wards. Our time was structured, leaving little opportunity for socializing with anyone except the people who were affiliated with the hospital or training program.

I was surprised to discover that I was the youngest male member of my class, and that the median age was somewhere around forty years old. With the passage of each day, I learned more about myself and other people, and the struggle for self-awareness, which is always ongoing. My negative qualities diminished, leaving the positive qualities intact. With the reinforcement from the class and firm and understanding input from the staff, I began to accept for the first time in my life that, in T.A. terminology, I was "Okay."

Back in Slaton, however, Susan and my daughters weren't doing as well. My wife got a job in Lubbock after completing a course in computer programming, while my mother kept our daughters. Although I'd maintained my sobriety for quite some time and tried to be supportive to Susan, our marriage suffered from my absence and Susan felt abandoned. She began seeing another man, and in my fifth month of training, she moved to her own apartment in Lubbock, leaving our children with my mother. I was so shocked and angered that I couldn't see that Susan was struggling with her own life and would have to find her own equilibrium.

After a painful confrontation one weekend when I was in Texas, Susan and I decided to file for divorce. Gathering my daughters and a few of their basic necessities, I returned to Colorado to complete school and be a single parent. It was a challenge that I was not sure I could meet, but one that proved rewarding to both my children and me.

One of my classmates in A.D.C.T.P. was a girl named Josie Baroz. She and her cousin, Diane Chacon, and I were close friends, and although I'd attempted to take Diane out once, I ended up asking Jo out instead. From then on Jo and I dated regularly and spent a lot of quiet hours together.

My apartment, which I'd rented for $65.00 a month, was a small, flimsy structure. It had a kitchen, bedroom, and bath furnished in Early Depression. The soiled, yellow walls were made of cardboard, I learned, after trying to wash one of them and having my washrag and hand go through the soggy area I'd been scrubbing. But the place took on a well-lived in look and was never dull. Since my duty-scheduling sometimes interfered with my fatherly responsibilities, Jo and Diane would baby-sit for me, usually taking the kids to their apartment several blocks away.

The girls missed home and their mother very much, so I decided to send them to my parents' care in Slaton. My divorce would be final with-in weeks, as it was uncontested, and I planned to return for the girls after I'd graduated that January and found employment. My best friend on the staff at A.D.C.T.P. was Dr. Louis Stephen, the chief research psychologist who taught the T.A. classes as well as ran long group sessions. It was with his encouragement and guidance that I was able to make many of the key decisions concerning my family's future.

As a child, I'd been overprotected by my mother during my asthma attacks, so I tended to be overprotective towards Stephanie and Amber. During the morning breaks and at lunchtime, I'd jump in my '65 Chevy and dash down the country road to the day care center "just to check on them." Dr. Stephen told me how I was living out a "script" from childhood, and how the kids needed their independence to adjust nor-mally.

After I'd taken them the four hundred miles to Slaton and returned to Fort Lyon, it came time to decide where I'd spend the last two months of training in the post-internship. There were numerous treatment centers from New York City to Sitka, Alaska from which I could choose. I wanted to be at a facility close to Texas. My father's health was deteriorating rapidly, and I feared being too far away, in case my mother needed me.

One weekend I drove to the San Luis Valley to see the Conejos County House of Help, near Antonito, Colorado, I fell in love with the beautiful country and the challenge that awaited me there, so I told the director, Sue Simmons, that I'd return for my post-internship. I also knew that Josie would be going there too, so our friendship and quickly-growing romance continued.

The San Luis Valley reminds me of northern Mexico. Located 125 miles north of Santa Fe, New Mexico, the valley sits above the seven thousand-foot level between the San Juan and the Sangre de Cristo Mountains. The people in our area were of mixed Indian and Mexican ancestry, as are Josie and her family. Most of the clients that came to the House of Help were impoverished, and had never known anything more than making a bare living out of seasonal work in the local produce fields.

Since the people in the valley had been abused for many years, be-ginning with the concerted efforts to drive the Ute Indians from their land in the mid-1800's, they had a strong distrust of whites. The intrinsic tragedy of these people touched me as I learned how wise they were. They had suffered pain and humiliation as well as loss of the land that was once theirs. And yet they still maintained a sense of patience and dignity.

Although the House of Help operated with some state funds, there was rarely enough money to pay the staff. The coordinators sometimes would forego their own salaries to enable their clients to eat, or just to pay the clinic's bills. Josie, Diane, and I were paid $100.00 a month with all meals furnished, but it was scarcely enough, considering that we were working up to seventy hours a week. Eighteen hour days were not at all uncommon. The peaceful surroundings of the trout streams and mountains were deceiving, since chronic alcoholism and drug abuse is high in the area. For the first time in my middle-class life, I was experiencing the cultural shock of poverty, as well as being an object of prejudice. It took quite a while for the people to trust me—to know that I sincerely believed in their capacity for change. I only wanted to help those who would accept it, and do little harm to those who would not.

I took a small apartment in Antonito and Jo moved in with me, scandalizing her family a bit. As the weeks passed, most of them recovered from their disapproval, and, for the most part, I was accepted into the family.

The coordinators were obsessed with their duties at the House of Help, and sometimes became very demanding and unreasonable. As in every situation where someone has absolute power, that power, at times, is abused. They manipulated each other and those around them—sometimes at the clients' expense. Since I was just an intern, I tried to stay clear of those hassles, but I did take the clients' side whenever it was evident that the program was hurting them.

When I first came to the House of Help, everyone working there were graduates of A.D.C.T.P., and, for a time, the staff seemed like an extended family. As time passed, more residents of the surrounding area of southern Colorado came into contact with our treatment regime. Consequently, the treatment facility, a renovated adobe house, became severely overcrowded. Since the largest contributor of funds to the House of Help was the State, I began to notice that many more clients were placed involuntarily and with little regard for the space available. Although the House was licensed for a maximum of ten patients, it became routine for its population to reach twenty or more.

Josie and I found a large old farmhouse near her uncle's ranch outside Romeo and rented it, since we expected a friend of mine to stay the winter with us. On a trip to my parents' home before Christmas, my friend, Jay Burks, and my oldest nephew, Casey, returned with us and a truckload of furniture. As long as there were four bedrooms for four people, things were calm. But soon the conditions began changing, as we began to accomodate the overflow of clients from the House of Help. I would return home after twelve hours of crisis intervention, emergency trips to clinics and hospitals over icy roads, and holding group therapy sessions, only to find our "home" filled with more people in need of attention. What was worse, Josie would have to face cooking supper for six or eight people at a time, and then clean up after them. We lived in a state of exhaustion.

One of the most rewarding experiences, however, was meeting Minnie Sutherland and her grandchildren, Shawn and Robyn Milligan. Minnie, a woman in her mid-fifties, lived in Manassa, Colorado; although she had close family ties, she was destitute and in the last stages of chronic alcoholism and emphysema. She and her "kids" lived from hand-to-mouth and my heart immediately went out to them.

After I spent six hours with Minnie one afternoon, I convinced her to go to the House of Help—just to look it over. When she agreed, we drove the eighteen miles to the center. Minnie didn't leave for several months. She ate some soup and slept in a clean bed that night, and the next week, after the agonies of withdrawal had passed, decided to stay the winter, eventually taking a partially-paid position as a cook.

Robyn and Shawn had other stories. When we first met, they'd been on their own so much that every act of kindness or gesture of concern was met with open hostility and sarcastic distrust. Robyn finally agreed to stay at the House of Help with Minnie, but Shawn was adamantly opposed to being there, so Josie and I took him into our home and helped him get back into school. Our house evolved into a communal residence, with people coming and going and their friends and families congregating, until our "treatment" began to rival that of the House of Help.

As bad as the conditions at the House of Help eventually became, it did help save lives. Many of the clients who sought treatment there would have died from exposure to the sub-zero temperatures of the area in winter, or of chronic alcoholism or pneumonia had it not been for the staff. Once, upon learning that a new client had been admitted, I went into the "detox" room to find an old Chicano vomiting fresh blood. His vital signs were dropping rapidly, so we loaded him into my car and raced to the nearest hospital, almost twenty miles away. The roads were covered with ice and snow. After a nerve-wracking drive, we finally made it.

Once Dr. Obie Minter examined the old man, and discovered a huge ulcer that had perforated and was bleeding profusely, we worked over the man, pumping ice cold water into his stomach, and pumping the bloody water out. After the bleeding had been controlled, we learned that he was a veteran but had never used his benefits. I was able to contact the Veteran's Administration Hospital in Denver and arrange for an emergency flight, since the old man would require surgery. Within six weeks he was home again with his wife and son. And now his family has hope, since he was found to be eligible for benefits he'd never claimed. This feeling of being instrumental in changing people's lives for the better made all the fatigue and frustration bearable.

The time Jo and I spent working in the San Luis Valley came to an abrupt end, however, and we moved to Temple, Texas. Our meager salaries had been cut for the second time in four months, and I learned that the House of Help couldn't reimburse me for almost $300.00 in personal car expenses. The House was losing so much money that it was forced to borrow just to pay back bills. It was pointless to continue there, even though we were needed. Leaving the snow-decked mountains and the people I'd come to know and love was hard but necessary. My children were still living at my parents' home six months after I'd graduated from school. In Temple, they could live with Jo and me and have a semblance of normality restored to their young lives.

FOUR

After leaving Colorado, I travelled to Temple with my mother before finding a job as an orderly in the Santa Fe Memorial Hospital, where my father was again a patient. I'd known the staff for years and after my train accident had been a patient there myself.

Jo and I took a two-bedroom apartment in Temple and my little girls rejoined us. Jo had a hard time adjusting to the sweltering central Texas heat, but, for the most part, we were a very happy family. My father and I spent ample time together while his health returned. He looked forward to living at home and taking it easy.

I enjoyed working at the hospital and knew many of the railhands who would come for annual checkups. Some were from my hometown and would carry messages back and forth from my parents. I was able to practice the counseling skills I'd developed, trying to convince the staff to establish an alcoholism and drug abuse treatment plan. A high percentage of the employees who entered the hospital had conditions directly linked to or aggravated by substance abuse. My suggestions were accepted, but I was told that until the company decided to begin a program system-wide, our hospital could do nothing.

After three months in Temple, a position opened up at the mental health clinic. I applied and was hired as a Resident Mental Health Worker, at "The Starting Place," which was the name of the adolescent unit at the Central Counties Mental Health/Mental Retardation Center. My schedule was similar to what it had been in Colorado. From 7 A.M. until 3 P.M. each day, I continued to work for the Santa Fe Hospital. Then I'd dash home, take a quick shower, and report for another eight hours at the mental health center. Initially, I felt capable enough to do this double-duty and was sure that both salaries, although small, would enable us to pay our debts. Josie hadn't had much luck in finding work, and we both began to feel that it may have been due to her race. The only positions that were offered her were menial jobs at stoop wages.

After a few weeks, however, I decided that I couldn't physically continue working both jobs, since caring for the teens at the drug center was taxing my strength. The orderly job paid less. So I resigned from the Santa Fe Hospital.

The longer I remained at the treatment center, the stronger became my bonds with the residents. We treated men and women from ages thirteen to twenty-two, admitting anyone we felt was serious about trying to improve his or her life. Some of the teens had been in trouble with the law, others were drug abusers, and some, having been abused by their parents, needed shelter and placement in foster homes. I shared my long struggle, and, in return, they gave me their trust and respect. This method was particularly helpful when my fellow staff members couldn't seem to get close to them. Working with Rick Lieberman, the Chief Psychologist, and Melanie Schockette, a graduate student, taught me a great deal about a more gentle, caring, and persuasive form of psychology than I'd used before. With their encouragement, I decided to pursue a degree in psychology since it was suddenly evident that my A.A. degree and training in A.D.C.T.P. was professionally limiting.

At the end of October, 1976, I received a phone call informing me that a new center had opened in Monte Vista, Colorado. The House of Help wanted Josie and me to return and operate the detox unit, which was located in the hospital in Monte Vista, and to supervise the halfway house across town. The salaries were too tempting to pass up, as was the thought of returning to Colorado. So, I obtained a leave of absence from the mental health center, and Jo, the children, and I returned to the mountains we loved.

When we arrived in Colorado and surveyed the facilities in Monte Vista, we were surprised and dismayed. The six-bed detox unit in the hospital was everything we would wish for in cleanliness and modern design. (The old detox room in the Conejos County House of Help was just a dimly-lit, spare bedroom lined with metal bunks.) Our new unit was actually two large hospital rooms on either side of a small, glassed-in office.

Although few people realize it, the withdrawal symptoms from alcoholism in its chronic stages can be more life-threatening and painful for the patient than heroin withdrawal. The vital signs must be constantly monitored and paramedical help made available in case of grand mal seizures or cardiopulmonary dysfunction.

Alcohol interacts with the body at metabolic, biochemical, physiological, and psychological levels. Ethyl alcohol is a very versatile pharmacological agent; although it is basically a physical depressant, it can also produce bizarre excitement. Biochemically, alcohol has the properties of both ether and glucose. Ether is an anesthetic and glucose an energy food. Alcohol produces heat energy but it provides no nutrition, so a patient who enters detoxification frequently needs restraining so he won't hurt himself. Chronic alcoholics can be undernourished and anemic, so they are high-risk candidates for disease and infection.

As pleased as we were, however, the halfway house was a disappointing sight. Scheduled to open only four days after our arrival, none of the beds were set up and the kitchen was without a refrigerator. Josie and I, with Teddy Cisneros' help, worked around the clock for three days in order to open the halfway house on schedule.

Our basic treatment plan differed from that of the House of Help. We agreed that, even with improved living conditions and a modern detox center, the best, short-term care we could provide on our limited budget was the removal of alcohol intake during detox, a physical exam, and psychological testing. We could accomodate, too, a short stay in the house, so the client's health could be rebuilt before discharge. It was evident that most of the clients wouldn't remain sober on their own, so essentially all Josie and I did while in Monte Vista was to buy them some time.

When the area supervisor job opened up, I stepped into it. I spent most of my time on the road again, travelling from the House of Help in Conejos County to the Rio Grande County facilities, sixty miles away. Occasionally, I made two trips a day or I'd be asked to conduct a workshop miles away in another part of the Valley or around the state. My duties also included contacting various law enforcement agencies, giving them information about our agreements with the state bureau and with several of the county courts. Given an alternative to incarcerating persons arrested for public drunkenness, the officers from outlying counties would bring these individuals to the detox center if there were no other charges pending against them. If the person was known to have a long history of alcoholism, then we would prepare involuntary commitment papers. These would hold the individual under the law for a thirty-day period of treatment and observation. For me, this was always a difficult decision since I didn't know how I'd feel if someone were to force me into a treatment center.

In January, 1977, Josie and I learned that the grant money for my salary had been cut, and that I had been working without pay for two weeks. The coordinators had known this, but hadn't mentioned it. Instead, they tried, without success, to have the Board of Directors create a new slot for me. The Board was agreeable, but there just wasn't any money.

We'd tried for the second time to bring a viable treatment center to the San Luis Valley, and for the second time we'd failed. Jo and I felt betrayed.

For the first time in over two years, I became extremely depressed and while driving around with a friend one night, I drank again. I continued to drink even after Jo and I moved back to Slaton later the next month. My father's health was declining and he asked me to come home. Jo and I moved into the mobile home that Susan and I had shared, even though the home needed repairs, since the pipes had burst and the roof leaked. My parents had assumed the note on the home, and the repairs I agreed to do were in exchange for several months rent. Papa told me that there was a lot of painting and repair work needed on our family home as well, and that they'd pay me equitable wages, knowing I'd do a good job.

Shawn Milligan, our young friend, returned to Slaton with Josie and me. He'd planned to seek work in west Texas, where anyone could find a job. Shawn helped me repair some of the broken pipes, but one morning as Jo and I were sleeping, we woke up to the sound of our bedroom door being smashed open. We saw three policemen, their guns drawn and pointed at us, standing in the room.

I learned that one of the patrolmen had driven by the mobile home and had seen Shawn walking around the side of the house. The place had been vacant for several months, and the officers thought that Shawn was a burglar. When one of the patrolmen approached Shawn, he resisted and the policeman drew his pistol and bludgeoned him in the face with the heavy magnum revolver.

The story sounded too patently rehearsed for me, but at the time there was nothing I could do. Although I tried to tell the police that Shawn was a guest of mine, they held him in custody anyway and charged him with resisting arrest. No apology was ever made for the damage done to our door—or for frightening Jo and me. I tried, without success, to talk to Shawn while he spent fifteen days in the county jail. We later learned that he had a completely different account of his arrest. From that point on, I was constantly harrassed by the local police, until I was finally arrested eight months later on a charge of murder.

After Shawn was released from the Lubbock County Jail, he returned to our house and told me that the policeman who'd assaulted him had driven up into the yard, stepped out of his patrol car, and yelled at him to stop. Shawn turned and approached the officer, but without another word or any warning, the officer drew his .375 magnum revolver and struck Shawn in the face. As the boy fell to the ground, the policeman hit him repeatedly—he could not say how many times—and, at one point, called Shawn by the name of "Brasfield." Struggling to his feet, Shawn tried to run, but was tripped by the patrolman as two other police cars pulled up. Together, they held Shawn in the dirt and handcuffed him. When he was turned over, however, one of the plainclothesmen told the others, "That's not Brasfield!"

The entire left side of Shawn's face was scarred and the sutures that closed the wounds were fresh and visible. After receiving emergency treatment, he was taken to Lubbock, charged with resisting arrest and sentenced. While in jail, Shawn was questioned several times by different men whom he believed to be officers from Lubbock. He was asked about my activities, where I'd come from and the name of the "Meskin" woman with me.

As confusing and frightening as Shawn's story sounded, I always believed him—in the two years I'd known him, he'd always been honest. Still, I couldn't understand why the police would be interested. I hadn't lived in Slaton for almost three years.

When Josie, Shawn and I talked it over, we decided it would be best if he went home to Colorado. Having hardly any money, all I could do was pay his back wages and take him to the west edge of Lubbock. From there he could hitch a ride to New Mexico, which lies about ninety miles due west. It was hard seeing the young man go, because he was a close friend, and I still felt responsible for him. The last thing his grandmother, Minnie Sutherland, had told me was, "Don't let anything happen to Shawn."

Josie and I told Papa and Ma about the problems we were having. We were confused. We'd barely been in Texas for three weeks, and already the all-too-familiar harrassment was starting again.

Both my parents felt that the police and a few politically-motivated "rednecks" (as my father called them) were responsible. My sister had remarried a black man and had had a child by him. Her oldest daughter was also married to a black man and had given birth to a beautiful little girl. Claire had once been married to an attorney's son, but the marriage hadn't worked out. I also knew this young man very well; his attorney father had blamed me for his son's drug abuse and had threatened to "get" me.

Papa told us, in no uncertain terms, that my sister and I had both broken the established social taboos which were still very much alive in our part of the country. He said that while it wasn't anyone's business, some people were so bound by those taboos that they'd *make* it their business. He asked Josie and I to be very careful where we went and not to go any place alone at night.

After returning to the mobile home, Jo and I decided that, as soon as possible, we'd save enough money to move. Once again, I couldn't pursue a college degree.

It was bitterly cold that March. The work I was doing on the broken pipes had to be done slowly since I didn't know a lot about plumbing. When Papa felt like it, he'd come down to the place and tell me what to do and how, but he would have to carry his oxygen bottle with him to breathe. Frustration was etched in his pain-filled eyes; at the age of sixty-two, his hands were almost useless, crippled and gnarled terribly by advancing arthritis. Eventually, however, we managed to get the pipes repaired.

Repainting my parents' home went just as slowly. It's a large, shingled house, and the dried paint had to be scraped off before the new finish could be put on. The inclement weather made working every day impossible. The longer we were in Slaton, the bleaker the outlook became. I'd never felt so isolated before, and Josie hated the flat, barren plains. We became closer in our despair and would sometimes just sit in the darkened mobile home, quietly talking.

On the last day of March, I was trying to get the top of the mobile home sealed before a storm front moved in. We'd painted the ceilings and didn't want to take a chance on more leaks spoiling our job. As I frantically tried to get the 950 square feet of roof painted, I ran out of sealant and had to drive to Lubbock for another can. Needing lumber as well, I stopped and picked up some used lumber and a few old tires to help anchor the mobile home roof.

Two weeks before, I'd met and talked with Claire's former brother-in-law, whom I'd known since he was a child, and, while talking with him, had learned that her ex-husband was living in Austin. According to this younger brother, the "ex" was "going totally out of his mind." I told him that I'd planned to go to Temple with my father when he went back to the hospital for another checkup, and would be glad to drive the extra thirty-five miles to Austin to look up his older brother. Not having the address with him, he told me to come by his home and get it the next time I was in Lubbock. So, since I was finally going to Lubbock, I decided to pick up the address. The rain I'd anticipated seemed to be holding off, and it was quickly becoming dark, so I knew I wouldn't be doing any more work on the roof that night.

When I arrived at their fashionable home on the west side of Lubbock, I didn't notice any cars in the drive, but stopped and rang the doorbell anyway. Just as I turned to leave, two of the younger children answered the door. I could tell that neither recognized me, so I told them I was "Jodi's uncle" (Jodi being my oldest niece's nickname). They both remembered me then and told me that their older brother wasn't at home. The nine-year-old said that he thought he knew where his brother was, but didn't know the address. I asked him for the directions, but the child said he could show me more easily.

We got into the truck and drove west for several- blocks, then went down other streets, traveling east and west, back and forth. It was evident that the boy didn't know where the house was that his brother was supposed to be visiting, so I stopped for gas, then took him back to his parents' home.

Where before there were no cars in front, now the street was packed with cars, including police cars! As we pulled up near the house, a patrol car blocked my path and an officer came and asked the boy if he was okay. The child said that he was and the policeman told me to wait

32

where I was as he took the boy indoors. As I was standing by my truck, three officers approached me and told me I was under arrest and started reading me my rights.

I was taken to the city jail and placed in a holding cell, where I waited for almost an hour before being told I was charged with kidnapping, my bond being set at $100,000.00!

I was totally unprepared for what they had said and asked to talk to the arresting officers, but was told they'd gone off duty; I could make a phone call if I wanted. I tried calling my parents but their line was busy, so I was placed back in the tank. Later, another officer allowed me to make a call, but it was too late, and as I didn't want to wake my parents and worry them, I called a bonding company in town. After explaining my predicament to the bondsman and asking him to call my parents in the morning, I went back to a cell and spent a sleepless night. I wondered why this had happened and how I could have been so stupid to ever go near that family again.

The next morning after I appeared at the arraignment, I was told that the charges of kidnapping had been dropped, but a charge of sexual abuse to a minor had been filed. I was aghast at the new turn of events, but felt somewhat relieved when I found out that the bond had been lowered to $10,000. After being transferred to the county jail, I spent another night in a cell. This one was designed to hold eight men, but there were eleven of us crowded together; some slept on the urine-stained floor. On April 2, the bondsman came to the jail and took me to his office where my mother and wife were waiting. After the papers were signed and an agreement reached that my mother would pay half the bond in cash and I would pay out the other half in weekly installments, the three of us drove home to Slaton.

The bonding company was owned by a family who at one time had been business partners with Mickey, my former brother-in-law. They allowed me to make this arrangement because of that connection, and I was extremely grateful, knowing that most bonds must be paid in cash. In addition to the cost of the bond, however, I was told to find an attorney. A week passed and we talked to an attorney who didn't take the case, but did tell me that it was unusual the child had never been examined by medical personnel. He also said the boy hadn't complained to the police himself, but that his older brother, the one I'd been looking for the night of the arrest, had. To confuse matters more, the complaint was signed by the youngster's mother.

After another week, my parents and I went to the office of Warren Goss, a prominent attorney who'd been recommended to us. After another meeting, Mr. Goss told me he thought the case would never be brought to court. His fee, in addition to the $500.00 retainer already paid him, would be $4,500.00 to be paid in weekly installments, like the remainder of the bond. Mr. Goss told me that the family was adamantly opposed to dropping the charges: they simply would not!

Needless to say, being unjustly charged with sexual abuse of a minor is very traumatic. The looks I got from the people in Slaton who had heard about the charges through the media were hard to endure, but I had no choice. I spent all of April and May painting my parents' house and doing more repairs both there and at the mobile home. After talking to an old friend from the Hispanic community, I landed a job at a local manufacturing company where he was employed. I was hired as an industrial painter, and while the pay was minimum wage, this was offset by not having to travel out of town, and having a steady income regardless of weather conditions. I spent all summer working there, and became friends with the foreman, Armando Ramirez, and another painter, Jerry Robinson. The three of us clowned around quite a bit and drank beer after working through the long, hot summer days. Our favorite spot was outside the city limits near a small row of stunted elm trees growing by a cotton field. The road was unpaved and rarely travelled except by area farmers. Jerry, Armando and I would go to "the trees" often, but usually I'd take my own transportation so I could leave when I wanted, not liking to stay out as late as they did. Jerry had yet to be married, and Armando seemed to spend little time at home.

At the end of summer, we were told that the job at the manufacturing company wouldn't last much longer. We'd spent months building and painting cotton harvesters which would now be used to gather the fall crops that blanket west Texas like fibrous fields of snow.

I began looking for another job and was fortunate enough to be hired by a man who, at one time, had lived across the street from my mobile home. The DeLeon family had lived there long ago when the stables and horses were on our property. Now there was only an empty barn, the greenhouse, and the mobile home.

The wages were much better at the carpenter's job, and, although winter was coming, Mr. DeLeon assured me they had plenty of inside work to tide his crew over. Fortunately, too, I could carpool to work each week, since another employee lived across from me and his son just lived down the block. Jo and I felt our luck was improving and we began to relax. The police were still following our truck around whenever Jo or I would go anywhere, or they'd park down the street and watch whoever came into or left our house.

Josie found a job as an aide at the local nursing home; with both of us working, I'd soon have the bonding company paid off and could begin paying the fee to Mr. Goss.

The carpentry work went well. I saw Armando and Jerry infrequently, but on occasion we'd get together for a few beers and idle conversation.

One day after work, I stopped by to see my parents and was shocked at Papa's appearance. He was short of breath, gasping for air with his fingertips turning blue, indicating a cyanotic condition. Ma was almost beside herself and I finally called the doctor, who came and examined Papa. As I expected, he felt that it would be best for my father to be taken to the Santa Fe Hospital in Temple. I didn't want my parents making the long trip alone, so I told them we'd leave the following mornning, unless Papa got worse. I called Dr. Holleman in Temple, gave him the details of my father's condition, and told him of our estimated time of arrival.

When I told Jo about the unexpected trip, she indicated that we only had about $8.00 on hand. I made a fast trip to my boss's home and borrowed an advance against my check. He wished me well and told me he'd say a prayer for my dad.

After the long drive the next day, we checked my father into the hospital, and my mother and I decided to stay until he was stabilized. In a consultation with Dr. Holleman, I learned that there was little hope for my father's recovery. His heart was severely enlarged and his aorta was aneurysmal. The weakened artery could rupture at any time. There was no hope for corrective surgery because of his emphysema. Dr. Holleman was sorry, but he knew from working with me the year before that I would prefer the news straight.

The day we left the hospital, I visited with Papa for almost an hour and listened to him as he told me how he'd provided for my mother, and how he expected me to always be supportive. He knew of his grave condition, too, and asked me to "kiss the babies for me, if I don't get to." I told him I planned to return in two weeks time, then we embraced and said goodbye, not knowing the next time I would be behind bars.

I stopped by the Mental Health/Mental Retardation center and briefly visited with my friend Melanie and a young man I'd known earlier who'd just returned to the program a second time. This was the only high point of a miserable, emotionally draining trip. The drive home was long and reflective, during which I gently told my mother what the doctor had said.

After returning home, I went back to work as usual, having the routine Josie and I were now accustomed to broken only by my nephew, Casey, coming home from the Air Force. It was good to have him with us, and his generosity was very touching. After he saw how broke we were, he gave us his Air Force wages.

I helped Casey find a job nearby our home, working in a cottonseed oil plant. With his help, Jo and I were sure we'd be able to get our bills paid, once and for all. I needed less than $100.00 to pay off the bond. Then, nine days after returning from Temple, the bondsman called my mother and told her that the lawyer had called them to say I'd better pay him something more on his fee or he'd go off my case. The caller told my mother to advise me to be in their office the next morning at 8:30 without fail . . . or they'd go off the bond and have me returned to jail.

The news astounded me, since Jo and I had religiously paid as much as we could every week during the summer and autumn. It seemed strange that the attorney didn't consider the retainer fee he'd been advanced, but there was no getting around it—I'd have to miss work and be at the bonding office the next morning. The following day would be October 26, 1977, the day Johnny Turner, Jr., would disappear from his parents' home and never be seen alive again.

FIVE

On October 26, 1977, I woke at 6 in the morning. Sleep just would-n't come that night because I was so worried about the possibility of going back to jail. The longest I'd ever been in jail before was three days.

After Josie, Casey, and I ate breakfast, I took them both to their jobs at 7 A.M., then returned home and washed the morning dishes, fed the cats and pet goat I'd bought for our daughters, and drove to Lubbock.

The bail bond office is in the old section of downtown Lubbock, on the east side; from Slaton, the easiest way to get there is by heading north on Avenue A past the warehouses and stockyards, then turning west on Broadway. Their office is one block over on Main Street, right across from the County Jail. That morning, however, Avenue A was snarled by slow-moving traffic, backed up several blocks due to some street repairs. So I cut across several blocks, hit Avenue H, and made it to the bail bond office a little past 8:30 A.M. as scheduled.

After talking with the staff there and telling them about the $500.00 retainer fee we had paid Mr. Goss several months earlier, the con-sensus was that I should get the receipt from my mother and return with it so the bail bondsman could check out my story. I suggested, instead, that they simply call Mr. Goss; but after trying and finding the line busy, I agreed to come back later in the day with the receipt, and, if possible, some money for the lawyer. Before I left, one of the staff members asked why I'd left the county without permission. For a moment, I didn't know what she was talking about, then realized that she meant my trip to Temple. After I explained the circumstances, she told me never to leave the county again without first getting permission. I agreed and drove back to Slaton.

My mother was relieved to see me come in the back door about 10:15 that morning, but became angry when I told her what the trip was about. She found the receipt for the $500.00, and I told her I wanted to pay the lawyer some more money so he'd get off my back. Although my parents were only then subsisting on a partial pension, she was generous enough to lend me $100.00. I told her I hadn't slept much the night before, so was going home to lie down before going back to the bail bond office to see the lawyer. Just before I left her house at 11:30 A.M., the phone rang and Casey asked her how Papa was doing. She told him she hadn't heard from him that week and asked if anything was wrong, but he told her no, he was "just calling," and hung up the phone. Neither of us could think of why he'd call out of the blue like that, but didn't think too much of it.

As I walked out, Mama reminded me that she'd be at an art class that afternoon if I needed her, and I told her I'd call if anything came up in Lubbock—but for her not to worry.

Before I went back to the mobile home, I drove to United Super Market and cashed the check, then went to a self-service gas station, filled the truck with gas, and checked the oil. Then I went home.

As soon as I drove up, I knew why Casey had called from work. The music from my stereo was blaring, and as I opened the door, there sat Casey grooving with the music, an embarrassed grin spreading over his face.

"I decided to play hooky half a day, Bub," he told me. Then he said his call was to pretend that he had to go home, so his boss would let him off. I told him I didn't care, but planned on taking a nap before going back to Lubbock later that day. He said that was fine; he wouldn't bother me and would wake me up about 1 P.M.

Much as I tried, I couldn't sleep very well and was reading a book when Casey tapped on the bedroom door. He'd fixed sandwiches for lunch, and after we ate, we sat around talking before deciding to get a six-pack. We also stopped by the grocery store for some chicken, since Casey had volunteered to fix supper.

After dropping him off, I went back to my mother's house and used the phone to tell the lawyer's secretary that I'd come by his office later that day. She told me I could see him at 4 P.M. I drove slowly to Lubbock and on the way, decided to stop by the new place where Jerry and Armando worked. I'd known the owner of the small construction company for many years, as he'd worked for the Santa Fe Railroad as the yardmaster in Slaton, and, at one time, had run for state representative.

I walked into the plant and saw Mr. Rose, the owner, talking to a man I recognized as an old schoolmate. Mr. Rose and I chatted awhile until I saw Jerry's car drive up outside. He and Armando were on a coffee break and had just returned from a nearby beer store.

I climbed in the car with them; sure enough, both were grinning ear-to-ear with cold cans of Coors wrapped in paper towels so Mr. Rose couldn't see what they were drinking. I told them about the hassle I was having with the lawyer and the bail bond people, and they agreed that it was a "drag" to have to deal with people like that. Jerry told me he was getting married the next day and asked if I wanted to "go get drunk" with Armando and him that night. I declined the offer, but invited them to my house for a few beers. I didn't want to risk driving around and drinking and probably getting taken to jail, if stopped by the police. They agreed to come over after work, and Armando said as I left, "We'll drive by your place after getting some beer, but if the truck's not there, then we'll make a run out to 'the trees' and come back later, bro'." So I drove to the lawyer's office, which was located on the corner of 13th Street and Avenue L.

After a short wait in his outer office, I was shown in to see Mr. Goss, and was taken aback when he asked me what he could do for me that day! After blurting out that I'd come to pay him because I'd been told he was vacating my case, Goss assured me that he'd never said anything of the kind, and if he had, it would have been directly to me and not through the bail bondsman. We talked a bit more and again he assured me about the case. Before leaving his office, I paid his secretary $80.00 and left for the bondsman's office.

As angry with them as I was, I contained my temper and simply showed the old woman who ran the office the receipt for the $500.00 and the new receipt for $80.00. She barely glanced at them and asked if I had any money for her! It was clear then—the phone call to my mother's house had been a ruse to scare me into paying more money. I told her I'd return with what money I could, but at the time I only had $12.00 to make it through the week.

I left her office and tore down Broadway to Avenue Q to catch the Loop to Slaton before the 5 P.M. rush hour. It only took me about thirty minutes to get home, and as I pulled into my mother's drive, I realized she'd just made it home herself. I gave her the receipts and told her the basic story, omitting most of the details about the phony call. When I happened to look up at the clock on the mantle, I told her I had to get home so Jo wouldn't worry, and because we had company coming that Jo didn't know about. I told Ma I'd see her the next day after work.

I knew Jerry and Armando weren't at work now, so after leaving Mama's, I went by the beer store and bought a six-pack on credit, then drove out of town about a mile and a half toward "the trees." Seeing they weren't there, I opened a beer and turned east on the first dirt road that would lead to the old Golf Course Road near the dump grounds that lie like an open sore on the lip of Yellowhouse Canyon. Turning back south then, I'd planned to drive to my house via a dirt road which ran by the cotton oil plant into the poor, ghetto section of Slaton called "The Flats."

I recognized Jerry's car about a half-mile away and revved my pickup to forty-five m.p.h., surprising them both as I drove up beside them and skidded to a halt, shaking my beer bottle at them invitingly. After talking a bit, they told me they'd come over to my place as soon as they picked up some more beer, since my six-pack wouldn't last.

When I drove into our drive, I saw our neighbors, Mr. and Mrs. Powers, standing in their yard, and waved, then went into the house. I don't remember exactly what time it was, but it was either just before or just after 6 P.M. since the news was on television. Casey was busily preparing supper and Jo was in the bedroom.

Neither Jo nor Casey seemed too pleased with the thought of company coming over, since Jo was tired and Casey hadn't prepared enough for everyone to eat. I told them Jerry and Armando probably wouldn't stay too long, and we could eat when they left. At that moment, Jerry's car pulled in front of our house and I let them in. They had two six-packs with them, so it looked like they'd planned on staying longer than I had anticipated.

The five of us sat around drinking beer, talking, and listening to the stereo until we ran out of beer about 8:30 P.M. Josie drove into town and bought more. Finally, Jerry left at 10:30, saying he didn't want to have a hangover since he was getting married the next day. We all laughed because Jerry was already past the point of avoiding a hangover. Armando stayed where he was, slouched on the sofa listening to a Freddy Fender album and singing drunkenly along with the Spanish lyrics until we finally ran out of beer again. Armando lived only three blocks away from our house, but Jo and I drove him home, then went in so Josie could meet his wife. We visited with them until almost 1 A.M., then went home and to bed after eating Casey's cold, ruined supper. The next morning before Jo and I left for work, Armando stopped by to pick up his tape measure that he'd left on our coffee table. We talked a bit on the front porch, then he and Jerry drove away. The next time I'd see either of them would be as they took the witness stand against me.

I worked that Thursday and Friday with the framing crew in Lubbock, but didn't draw a check since my wages went to pay Mr. DeLeon for the advance I'd received. That weekend, Josie and I took part of her paycheck to the bail bond office and paid them another $25.00, then went to Texas Instruments, Inc. so Josie could fill out an application form to be hired and trained to build calculators.

On Thursday, we began to hear the sad news that a black child, six years old, had either strayed or been kidnapped from his parents' apartment in northeast Lubbock. All the radio stations, television networks, and the *Lubbock Avalanche Journal* were giving the search wide coverage. Sunday night there was a tearful appeal from the little boy's mother for the return of her youngest child. As Josie and I watched, she said she didn't know what she'd do if Stephanie or Amber were to disappear like that. I agreed that it must be an unbearable nightmare, and felt somewhat glad that the girls were in Dallas visiting with their mother and new stepfather for two weeks.

On Monday, Halloween, before I took Jo to work at the nursing home, I noticed that our front right tire was going flat. We drove slowly to a service station on the way to her job and inflated the tire. I told Josie I'd ride to work with Edward DeLeon and would bring the truck back to her once I took it home and put on an old spare tire. She said she'd get the good tire repaired later that afternoon and for me to be careful at work that day. We embraced and went our separate workaday ways, never knowing that fate was intruding on us with increasing force.

I went home and quickly changed the tire. Edward followed me to the nursing home where I left the keys for Jo, who was busy with one of her patients. Arriving in Lubbock, the crew and I worked all day. I caught a ride home after 5 P.M. and had just taken a shower when Jo came in breathlessly.

"Oh, I didn't know you were home," she said. I told her that I hadn't been home very long. Then she said that as she'd driven into the yard, an unmarked police car with four men in it had driven up behind her and asked if she knew where I was. She'd told them I was probably still in Lubbock or on my way home.

I had no idea what they wanted, and Josie said that one of the policemen had told her that they wanted to find out where Shawn Milligan was living now, so they could clear up some paperwork. Neither of us had any idea where Shawn was; I'd received only one short letter since February with a Colorado Springs return address.

As I finished dressing and drying my hair, I heard a knock on the door and, slipping into some moccasins, opened the door and greeted a Slaton sergeant I recognized as being one of the men involved in Shawn's arrest. Asking him in, I quickly learned that he indeed did want Shawn's address, so I went into the bedroom to get the letter. After rummaging through a desk drawer, I found the worn envelope, copied the address for the officer, and handed him the small sheet of paper. I asked him if there was anything else he wanted, and he told me that the men in the car wanted to talk to me outside.

Expecting more harrassment, I told him I'd rather they come into the house—or, if need be, I'd finish dressing and come to the police station after Jo and I had finished supper. The sergeant assured me that it wouldn't take long to talk to the men, so, motioning to Jo to follow me, I walked out to the blue sedan parked in our drive.

I climbed in the front seat and immediately felt something was wrong by the expression on the officers' faces. You could smell their tension underneath the cheap shaving lotion that permeated the close, hot air in the car.

The driver identified himself as a detective sergeant of the Lubbock Police Department, and introduced me to his partner and to another officer who was in the back seat. The detective asked me where I'd been on Wednesday, October 26, 1977, and I began telling him that I'd been to Lubbock twice that day, had seen an attorney, and had been to the bail bond office twice. Other than that, I'd either been at home or at my mother's house.

When I finished, the sergeant's face swelled in anger and turned a deep red; he hissed through clenched teeth, "We know where you were, you son-of-a-bitch. We can put you in Lubbock at the same time Johnny Turner disappeared and we can get a positive identification from people who saw him with you."

I was totally stunned by what I'd just heard and barely heard one of the officers in the rear seat tell me my Miranda rights. "You have the right to remain silent, the right to an attorney being present while you're questioned . . . ." The detective removed a set of handcuffs from his belt and secured them on my wrists; tapping the horn, he motioned the Slaton sergeant who'd lied to me over to the car.

"We got him," the detective said. "C'mon, we're taking the mother-fucker to the station." The Slaton man walked away from Josie, with whom he'd been talking near the front gate, and as he opened the door, I yelled at her to contact my lawyer and then come down to the police station. The agonizing expression on her pretty face was painful to see.

As we drove away, I thought how ironic it was that this was Halloween: the goblins came calling, all right, but gave me a trick rather than a treat.

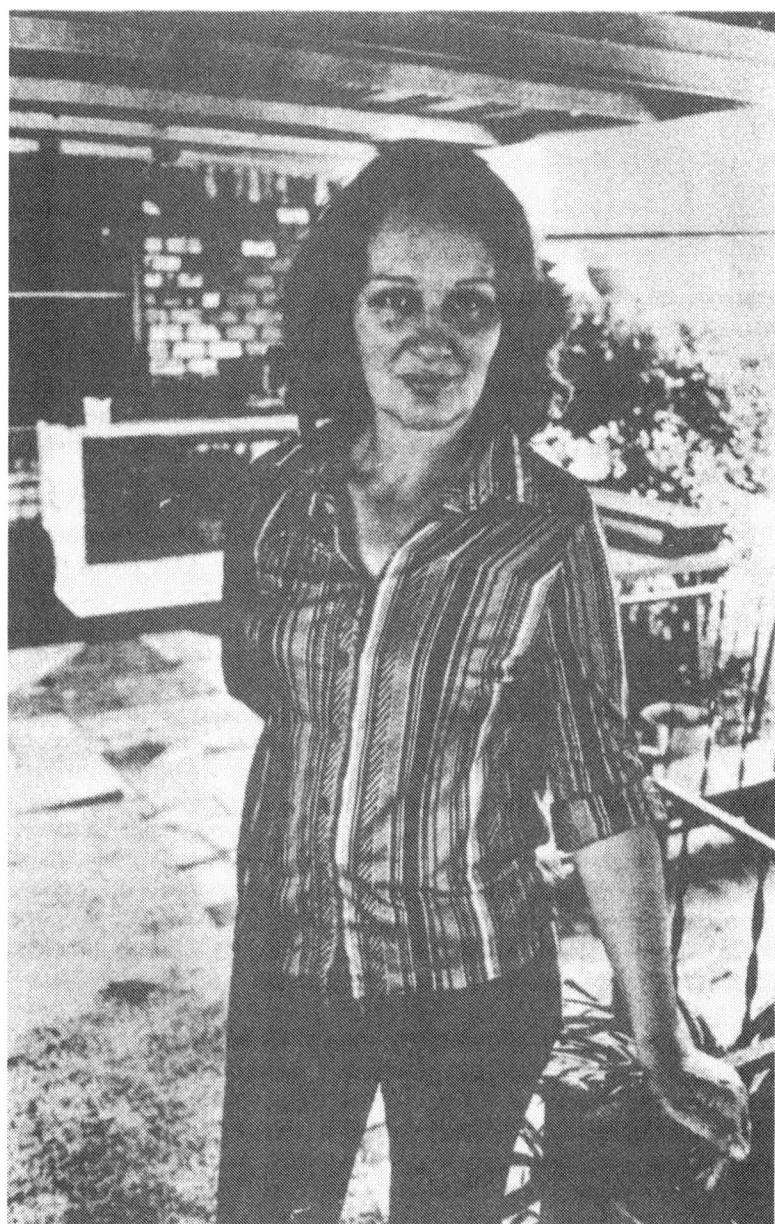

SIX

None of the officers said anything further until we arrived at the Slaton police station. Walking into the lobby, we passed by several people standing on the sidewalk. A woman was kneeling beside two small children and pointed in my direction, telling them, "That's the bad man daddy was looking for." I assumed she was one of the policemen's wives and that my arrest had been a source of gossip at the local department that day.

I was escorted into the sergeant's office and told to sit down. The detective began his questions; I again described my actions on October 26, 1977. Over the next few days I would repeat my story both to this detective and to several other officers many, many times, and never see them accept the simple truth.

After Josie arrived, she was kept for a few minutes while my mug shots were taken. For a moment, I believed I was going to be held in Slaton, but then was told I would be taken to the Lubbock City Police Station later that night. Before the sun went down, one of the rookie officers asked the detective if he wanted pictures taken of our white pickup, and was told that this was a good idea.

Before leaving for Lubbock, Josie and I had a very brief chance to embrace one another, and as she hugged me, I whispered to her to get the valuables out of our mobile home, believing that once the news of my arrest made the television stations, hoards of curious people might drive by to gawk at the place or even burglarize it. Jo told me she didn't want to stay there alone, and we agreed that she and Ma should stick close together.

Even after repeating to the detective that I wanted to see my attorney and telling him over and over again that I couldn't tell him anything about the disappearance of Johnny Turner, Jr., he kept questioning me. Before reaching the Lubbock Police Department, he told me that when the boy's body was found, he would personally take me to wherever it was so the news media could film it. I wondered how the man could be so sure that the little boy was dead when nothing but his tragic disappearance was evident. It was after dark when we arrived at Lubbock, and pulled into the covered parking lot connected to the police station. Entering through the back door, we climbed a steep flight of stairs and entered the detective's bleak office. The officer who'd been silent was told by his boss to take my photographs and contact the "eye witnesses" before setting up a lineup. I was allowed to call Mr. Goss, but only reached his wife, who told me he was on his way to the station.

When Mr. Goss arrived, the officers left us alone and we discussed the day's events. He told me I didn't have to volunteer another word to the police unless I chose to, and actually advised against it.

Goss asked if I'd done much "time" before, and I told him I hadn't. So he explained that the police would probably harass me while they could and I had to be as strong as possible. He told me that the lineup was being planned, and that he'd talk to me after it concluded.

After he left the office, the detective returned with a set of soiled, white jail clothes, and ordered me to strip and leave my jeans and shirt in his office. After I dressed, he led me to a smaller office where a two-way mirror ran halfway up one wall. Standing around the office were four other men of varying ages, all wearing dingy, white jail clothes. I didn't know if they were really prisoners from the county jail or policemen at the time, but later learned they were prisoners who had received cigarettes, phone privileges, and coffee in exchange for participating in the ritual lineup.

I was clearly the tallest of the other four men, and, while we were all dressed alike, I was the only man there with a full beard. If the "witnesses" had been shown photographs of me taken before the lineup, as I believe they had, then it would be a cinch for them to pick me out from the other four.

I was told I could stand anywhere I wanted, and then, after one of the alleged "witnesses" had finished looking at us, I was allowed to change places in the line if I wished. I moved one space over, thinking what a charade the whole thing was in view of the contrasting appearances of the other men with me. I stuck out like a sore thumb.

The lineup completed, we were shuffled out into the hall where a group photograph was taken. The other men in white left down one hall and I was taken back to the detective's office, where I sat alone, smoking. I hadn't thought enough to bring my pipe when going out of my house a few hours before to "talk" to the men waiting for me.

Fifteen minutes later, Mr. Goss came into the office. I could tell by his pale complexion and jumping jaw muscles that something was wrong. "They made you," he told me. I didn't know what he meant, so he explained that at least one of the witnesses had said she was positive of the identification. *Only* she had been positive, he continued. The other two had said that there was only a resemblance, but couldn't be absolutely sure. My heart sank as Goss told me that the police could and would hold me over on the basis of this identification. Just then I heard my mother's voice in the hallway demanding to see me. Before I could ask him, Mr. Goss rushed out of the room and intervened in the confrontation that was developing between the idle officers standing outside the door and my mother and wife.

A short while later, Goss returned and told me he'd see me the next morning at the arraignment; he reminded me I had nothing to gain by talking to the officers anymore.

For the next two hours, the detective tried different ploys designed to either frighten or provoke me. He'd rant and rave in my face, just inches away, then step out of the office while his partner became either patronizing or conciliatory. It was an incongruous display of the "good guy/bad guy" police sketch with which television viewers are so familiar. Their act was perfect.

At midnight, he grew angrier at my inability to tell him what he wanted to hear, and agreed with the other officer to call it a day. I was taken downstairs and booked on charges of kidnapping. While I tried to answer the questions that the booking officer asked, the detective interrupted, telling him I was unemployed (when, in fact, I wasn't), telling him I was divorced (when he knew better), and supplying other false information later published in the local newspaper as "the truth."

At the time, the city jail in Lubbock had only a few "tanks" where town drunks, traffic violators, illegal aliens, and others were placed. The walls were made of heavy gauge steel and there were two rows of steel banks running around three sides of the cold, damp place.

I was alone in the tank, however, and the only other thing in there besides me was half a roll of toilet paper, a styrofoam cup, and a dog-eared copy of *Star Wars*. My light and the cigarettes the police had given me had been taken away when I was booked. For the next eight hours I walked the length of the tank, stopping only to accept hand-rolled cigarettes from one of the illegal aliens being held in the tank next to mine. He'd roll the smoke, light it, and stick it through the steel mesh wire that ran around the top of the cells. We could barely talk, his English being as bad as my Spanish, but I'm sure the gratitude I showed him was understandable. His was the only kind face I'd see that night.

After he went to sleep, I paced back and forth, armed with the small stack of cigarettes, single matches, and a piece of striking pad he'd given me. The mattresses had been removed from the tank I occupied, so sitting was painful; the cold, hard steel made sleeping impossible, even if I could have slept. I paced, smoked, and prayed.

Breakfast consisted of two slices of white bread, a cold fried egg, and a bitter cup of coffee. I left the egg sandwich lying on the bunk and drank the coffee. Suddenly, I heard the key slam in the heavy lock and someone bark the name "Brasfield." After being let out of the tank and walking to the booking desk, I saw the two arresting officers standing there with a set of handcuffs lying on the counter. We were going to the arraignment, I was told, and after the cuffs were placed tightly on my wrists, we drove to the county courthouse a few blocks away. The sand was blowing out of the north. The cold November wind blew right through my thin jail clothes and made me shiver.

I was totally unprepared for the six officers in uniform who were waiting for us at the courthouse, and for the gaggle of newsmen, cameras, and other media paraphernalia that accosted us as we stepped off the elevator. Walking past them, I kept my head held high and never averted my gaze. I had nothing to hide, but I was antagonized by the crowd and I was frightened. The courtroom fell silent after Mr. Goss and I spoke a few words. The Justice of the Peace briefly read the charges, asked me if I understood them, and inquired how I would plead to the charge of kidnapping. "Not guilty, your honor," I said.

Bond was denied at the request of the District Attorney's office. I was taken to the elevator again and we drove back to the city jail, facing an entire day of questioning by police and other interested parties, including two former acquaintances from my years in public school.

That afternoon, after not being given anything to eat, I was told by Jerry and Armando's employer that, while he didn't understand how I could have done such a thing, he'd get down on his knees and pray with me if I'd only confess and tell him where the little boy's body was so they could give it a decent burial.

That was it. I'd reached my limit. I couldn't cope with the circus atmosphere around me. I angrily told him to leave me alone, get out of the office, and stop trying to share in the limelight of this tragedy. He flushed, then composed himself, and made an attempt to remind me of his "friendship" to my family and his promise of future prayers. When the detective came in to see why I was shouting, I told him I would never say anything further to anyone. I never did.

Before being taken to county jail, where I'd stay for the next four months, I almost stepped into a death trap. It was later that afternoon. I was sitting in the booking room, waiting for the two officers to bring their car around to the back entry. A uniformed patrolman came in and kept passing near me, pacing back and forth, coming nearer each time. I noticed the snap on his holster was unsnapped.

He was purposely paying no attention to me, which in view of my sudden notoriety, caused me to feel that something was wrong. Looking around me, I suddenly felt cold; another officer was standing right behind me with a sawed-off shotgun in his hands, his eyes glaring at me with hatred.

"Nice try, fellas," I said, "but it's not gonna work." Both cursed me before they walked out of the area, one saying, "That's all right, punk, you'll make a wrong move one of these days and we'll be there waiting."

The detective and his partner left after I was booked into the Lubbock County Jail. I immediately noticed that the extreme animosity which the city police had shown me wasn't as evident in the sheriff's deputies, who were more businesslike and polite. The only complaint I had at the time was being placed in a cell on the first floor between two black prisoners. When they recognized me from the television coverage, they began to curse, threaten, insult, and harass me, which lasted until Mr. Goss and another attorney, Mark Hall, came to see me that day after the evening meal—the first I'd had in over twenty-four hours. While we tried to talk, the lawyers saw how the blacks were behaving and requested that I be placed in a security cell on the third floor.

All three television stations had aired pictures of me in court, and the extensive coverage included updates on what was being billed as the "most heinous crime" and the most extensive search in the county's history. Law enforcement officers and volunteers were searching for the body of the child in the city, the county, and the canyon area near Lubbock. There was little hope he'd be found alive, and there was talk of racial trouble in the east side of Lubbock. The victim was black and helpless; the alleged perpetrator was white and stocky.

The three prisoners in the security tank already knew who I was. Each came by the cell and by way of introduction told me what they were charged with: one with burglary, another with bank robbery, and the other with more serious offenses. His name was Clarence Allen Lackey, he was a strapping twenty-three year old, and he'd been charged with the rape and murder of a Texas Tech University Medical Center secretary.

I suddenly knew how he felt, because in July the news media had given his case as much coverage as I was now receiving. I also remember feeling anger over the slaying of the young woman and thinking to myself that the guy charged with it must be an animal. The realization was chillingly clear: others in the South Plains area would now think the same, if not worse, of me.

* * * * * *

It was wishful thinking to believe that I'd not be harassed by the detective sergeant again. That night, he and his partner came to the jail and took me to their car, where they tried once more to "break" me. It was incredibly frustrating to deal with individuals who simply wouldn't listen to anything I said; they were already convinced I was the person responsible for the little boy's disappearance. After almost two hours, I was taken back to the county jail and returned to my cell, where I sat up most of the night, unable to sleep because of threats made against my wife and mother.

The threats made by the police officers were indirect: What did I think would happen when the blacks found out where my wife was, and what did I think the blacks would do to my mother and wife? (They always used the term "nigger" even when talking about the Turner child.) The truth was, however, there had already been threats made against me by anonymous phone callers to the police and sheriff's offices. Knowing that the mood of the city was like that of a lynch mob, I was concerned that someone might harm my family. At least my daughters were out of the area.

The next morning, November 2, 1977, both officers were back even though my attorneys had told them not to bother me anymore. While we sat in the Jail Captain's office, a call came in: a search team had located the body of Johnny Turner, Jr. The detective came in with tears in his eyes and told his partner that the boy had been found, then screamed at me that he was dead. They hurried out and I was returned to my cell, only to be taken out later and escorted under a six-man guard to the courthouse.

Once there, I was charged with the capital murder of Johnny Turner, Jr., while the video cameras recorded it all and the growing crowd looked on in silence. Walking back through the tunnel to the jail, one of the armed guards asked if I knew why I was under such heavy protection. I told him I'd heard that there had been threats made against me. He replied, "More than threats, Brasfield. One of those niggers is gonna get you. I just hope you don't expect any of us to do much to stop it." Another patrolman on the other side of me said, "It wouldn't be such a bad thing. We could get rid of a few niggers and scum like him in the process." It sickened me to hear the way these alleged "protectors of law and order" were talking—even more than the words I'd heard in court. The only thing I could do was remain silent through the remainder of the verbal harassment and find solace in prayer. I hadn't done that in a long time, but I'd begin to do it more and more until, in the middle of all the fear and anger and confusion, I'd find a refuge from which I'd never let go.

When I was taken back to 3-3 Tank, put in my cell, and locked away that afternoon, I was at the lowest point of my twenty-eight years. No one but a handful of my family knew that I was telling the truth about my activities on October 26th, and it appeared that few people, if any, in the law enforcement field cared. As darkness fell outside and the other three men in the tank left me alone, I lay on the hard mattress and thought about taking my own life, sparing myself any more of the ordeal that was just beginning to unfold. I lay there all night long, my third day with little or no sleep and very little food, and cried silently from utter, devastating despair. A depression came over me that I couldn't shake for days. I trembled constantly and couldn't hold down any food. I slept fitfully, wakening from terrible nightmares in which the police were torturing me or chasing me down dark corridors. The first two weeks of my long incarceration passed like this, and there was no respite, not even when my mother and wife visited. There was also no relief from the cautiously-optimistic words of the attorneys the court had appointed to replace Warren Goss: Mark Hall, a young lawyer with little experience; and Dennis McGill, who was associated with a prestigious law firm, would handle my case.

As much as we wanted to keep the news from my ailing father, he had to be told before some of the well-meaning railhands going to Temple would see him. My mother called, and when she told him, Papa immediately said he wanted to come home and do what he could to help. Ma and Jo drove down and picked Papa up against the doctor's orders so he could be there to help, if possible, over the Thanksgiving weekend.

My depression began to wane with a visit from a small man with a Bible. I woke up one morning and saw Clyde Thompson standing on the other side of the bars near my bunk. After we exchanged a few pleasantries, Clyde left his book, *The Only Way Out Is Up*, and then left. I continued to feel sorry for myself and my family, feeling like an animal caged for a crime I knew nothing about. At that time, the only dialogue I dared conduct with God was to curse Him for allowing this to happen to my family who were unraveling under the constant strain. I prayed, but I prayed to die or prayed for a chance to escape and run away to a place where I couldn't be found.

In the weeks ahead, Clyde would stop by the jail and visit with me and listen patiently. He knew what I felt, since he had once been sentenced to death and spent twenty-seven years in prison before being paroled. He told me—and more importantly—his actions showed me, that, indeed, the only way out would be up—through the strength I would find from God, whom I began to trust again.

November passed with a few visits from my lawyers. They would come and reassure me and ask questions, utilizing a private investigator to check out "leads" that eventually led nowhere. It was too early to plan strategy for the trial, I was told, but they continued to encourage me.

December was by far the worst month. While the three other men played endless games of checkers and watched their television sets, I remained in my cell, reading or writing. Christmas day was terrible for all of us that year. For those in jail and their families and loved ones, the day must have been as bleak and heartbreaking as mine was for me. As I lay there shivering on Christmas night after watching Midnight Mass on television, I couldn't help but think how bad the Turner family must have felt, having lost their young son.

I was slowly finding an inner peace through my tenuous walk with God, faithful that He would know far better than I what was best for me. But my old self wished that whoever was responsible for Johnny Turner's death would be apprehended so that my ordeal would end. My antagonism for that faceless, formless individual was as great as the love I have for my family. It would only be a few days, however, until I experienced the shock and pain that caused me to excise all remaining thoughts of hatred from my mind.

My parents and wife came to visit me one day, and it was both good and painful to see my father. He looked like he'd aged ten years since I'd taken him to the hospital almost two months before. The jailer was kind enough to allow him into the small hallway in front of the cell so we could talk. Usually, the visitors were kept in the lobby of the third floor and had to shout through small speaker vents to be heard. Papa's voice was so thin—and he had such a hard time breathing—that he could barely talk above a whisper. The time we stood there holding one another's hands through the bars crying was so emotionally draining that I couldn't do anything after they left but lie down and cover myself with blankets so the others in the cell wouldn't see my tears. Before Papa slowly walked out of my sight, he told me he believed in my innocence, admonishing me to "be strong."

The following Sunday was New Year's Day, January 1, 1978. Clyde visited, and the jail served us a decent meal, as they had for Thanksgiving andChristmas. That afternoon we were all allowed a short, ten minute phone call and I talked briefly to Josie and Ma, then for the remaining minutes to Papa. I told him I'd written him a letter and that I'd call him again Wednesday, our regular day for phone calls. In my letter I'd told him about how I'd found inner peace through Jesus, and how he and Ma didn't have to worry about me, no matter what the future might bring. Later, Ma told me that the letter made him happy and he felt like I'd finally found what I'd been looking for.

On Wednesday evening, at 6:30, I was called out of my cell for a visit with my attorneys. Expecting to see Hall and McGill, I was surprised that Warren Goss was standing in the littered hallway. "Phil, I'm afraid I've got some bad news for you," Warren said. I thought he was going to tell me that a motion pending for a change of venue had been denied, so I wasn't expecting for him to say, "Your father died about an hour ago at home, Phil. Your mother asked me to come and tell you. I'm very sorry for all of you."

My father was dead. I couldn't or wouldn't believe it. I'd just been thinking of him a few minutes earlier and been looking forward to the phone call I'd expected to make. I grabbed myself around the shoulders, and fighting back an agonizing scream of rage and pain that was bursting in my mind, I slid down into a sitting position on the floor until I regained a measure of self-control.

Before Mr. Goss left, he arranged for me to use the phone. Ma answered, and we consoled one another, she more than I when she told me that Papa had died in her arms, that it was a peaceful death and that he hadn't suffered.

My former wife and our children had been visiting them, and he'd lived long enough to see them and me, too, which he had wanted very much to do. Stunned beyond words and unable to comfort her any further, I told her I'd call again as soon as I could. Before hanging up, she asked if I would tell Josie, who was at work and didn't yet know. I told her I'd call, and then numbly hung up the phone.

Jo was surprised to hear from me. It was unusual for anyone to call her at work and more unusual for me to call, since the regular Wednesday phone calls were limited to five minutes. I could almost see her face crumple when I gave her the bad news, and for minutes we simply cried, listening to one another's sobs, yearning for the reinforcing touch, the embrace of condolence that we knew we couldn't share.

After leaving the phone and telling some of the inmates that my father was dead, they thoughtfully left me alone and turned down the televisions in their cells. I lay in the darkened cellblock, alternating prayers for Papa's soul and my family with tears of abject grief. One by one, the jailers and guards from other sections of the jail came by to tell me they were sorry. I was touched by their sincerity. An old school friend, Steve Eddings, who was working temporarily at the jail, spent several hours with me that night, as we talked about the past, the present, and the unknown future. I remembered how hard it had been for Steve when his father, also a railhand, had died.

I thought about my sister, whose birthday had been the day before our father's death. How badly she must have felt. The next day, Ma and Josie came to see me, telling me about the funeral arrangements and how difficult it had been to get permission for me to visit the funeral home. The district attorney had flatly refused their request for me to attend the funeral. His reason: security.

But I was able to view my father's body with my family. This gathering, in such pain, would be the last one for us all. I couldn't return the innocent embraces of my children or my great-nephew because my hands were shackled to my waist. I could only give my family what love I had through words of encouragement, words that came not from me, but from the Lord to whom I had prayed for strength.

Alone for a few minutes with my father's body, I looked at his features in detail so as never to forget that handsome face. The lines from the years he'd spent toiling for his family were now smooth. He seemed at peace. As the deputies led me out of the room and past my weeping family, I remembered the last words I'd heard Papa say: ''Be strong!''

SEVEN

I was emotionally cauterized on the return drive. The deputies attempted to make small talk; one offered me a cigarette, but I declined. I wanted to be left alone. My feelings must have been evident, because after we arrived at the jail and I changed clothes again, back into the white, baggy pants and the thin shirt marked "County Jail," the guards and prisoners gave me wide berth and left me with my own personal thoughts.

As much as I was hurting, I realized my mother and the rest of the family was feeling as much, if not more, pain. I had to give them support. After all, it would only be a few short weeks until the trial began, which would be another enervating experience for us all.

My father's funeral was held at 2:30 P.M. As the time passed, I lay in my cell, covered with dirty blankets, thinking of him, my mother and my family, hoping they knew my prayers and love were with them.

The following Sunday, Josie and her mother, Janet Stewart (who'd flown in from Alaska), came to see me at the jail. The weather had turned colder and more snow was forecast. Seeing my mother-in-law was uplifting because she is an ardent believer in God, and during the thirty or so minutes we were allowed to talk, we prayed together. I asked God for help to be strong. It almost didn't matter anymore that lifelong friends, or those I thought were friends, and members of my family (uncles, aunts, cousins), didn't write or stand by me when I needed them. The old adage one hears in jail, "You sure know who your friends are once you come here," seemed true. Yet, I understood their reluctance and accepted the difference between real friends and mere acquaintances. It was enough to have my small family and Clyde Thompson. Another Christian, Grace Batt, came regularly, too. She cared simply out of Christian love, which, when sincere, is one of the most powerful forces on Earth.

On January 19, I called my former wife, talked briefly to my daughters, and then learned from Susan that my former brother-in-law had been shot five times and seriously wounded in Denton, Texas.

The details were vague—apparently he and his present wife had argued, he'd become violent, and she'd shot him to avoid being beaten as my sister had so many times when married to him. The forces of violence were attacking my family from all sides.

Later that week, my attorneys came to see me for the first time in three weeks, and told me about the pretrial hearing for the change of venue. As we talked, they indicated that the State's evidence was circumstantial and weak. The chemist from the Texas Department of Public Safety had been unable to find a shred of physical evidence on my truck that would somehow tie me or it to the location of the child's body or the child himself. Both lawyers seemed genuinely surprised at the news, but I wasn't, since I'd never seen the little boy before.

At the pretrial hearing, the defense made a motion for the trial to be held outside Lubbock County, since the pretrial publicity was negative and intense. Alton Griffin, the District Attorney, joined in the motion which Judge William Shaver readily granted. However, my heart sank when I heard the location: Wichita Falls, Texas, which was more conservative and more law-and-order oriented than Lubbock County could ever hope to be. Additional motions were made and granted to administer electroencephalographic tests in case I'd suffered organic brain damage during the train accident almost four years earlier. The other motion dealt with having a psychiatrist examine me at a later date to see if I was capable of standing trial. I felt that both examinations were unjustified, a waste of time and money, but I had no choice but to comply.

On February 1, I took the EEG test, which had to be done twice. The next morning, I was taken back to the Methodist Hospital for a longer series of tests called an "EMI." I was placed in a reclining seat that was attached to an enormous machine. It looked like something out of a science-fiction movie. The technician explained to me, as he positioned my head in a cup-like device, that the EMI test was a series of brain x-rays taken in sections. From it they could see if there were any lesions or tumors. I lay very still as the swimming cap-like covering on my head filled with cold water and tightly squeezed my skull. The entire test lasted only thirty minutes, although the sensation that time had completely stopped was very real.

I had only one more conference with my lawyers, and I didn't see them again until after I returned from Wichita Falls, where I was taken for the psychiatric exam given by Dr. Richard Bibb. The drive to Wichita County was surprisingly pleasant, because the assigned deputies treated me normally instead of acting superior to me. Before the trip, one of the men told me he'd like to establish a gentleman's agreement: "You don't run and I won't shoot you in the back!" I didn't argue, and only wished that the other officers would come off their "macho" acts and see me for what I was: just another human being. I hated being considered a threat to anyone, but instead of showing my anger, which would only reinforce their opinions, I vowed to go along with the petty rules. I felt, and still feel, that a man's behavior will eventually speak louder than what anyone has said about him or assumed to be the truth about him—even if he has been labeled a criminal.

Our society is quick to assign people labels that immediately set them apart from the whole. If you take a man or woman off the street, accuse them of a crime, dress them in county-issued clothes, and then lock them behind a steel cage, they aren't considered human any longer, but something less. Our law states that a person is innocent until *proven* guilty, and, in theory, that's a noble ideal. In practice, however, it's often just empty words. As the days passed, I came to understand how people in state institutions become so utterly embittered towards authority.

In my own case, the news media had played such a prominent part in giving the public subliminal messages of my guilt, that the trial had to be moved. Two of the three television stations continued to show me being led into the courtroom for the reading of the initial indictment several times a day, using this stock footage as an advertisement for their evening news program. The dramatic music, the serious voice-over saying "Action News," and short flashes of on-screen disasters, were followed by a five-second segment of my attorney and I walking into the courtroom. Innocent until proven guilty? I wonder how many people in the viewing area around Lubbock County felt that way after weeks of this kind of coverage.

Once I arrived in the Wichita County Jail and the deputies from Lubbock left for their motel rooms, I waited in the drunk tank, expecting to be taken to an isolation cell. As the night wore on and the putrid tank filled with local drunks, I became increasingly worried that there had been a breakdown in communications between my attorneys and the jail.

At 11 P.M., the officers started handing out worn, soiled blankets to the sobering drunks, and I learned that they had no knowledge of any arrangement for a private cell. I'd have to spend the night before the psychiatric examination surrounded by quarrelling, hung-over, physically-ill alcoholics. I had to sleep either on a bare, wooden bench or on the filthy, urine- and vomit-covered floor. All night long, I sat erect, smoking hand-rolled cigarettes, and trying to ease the cramps in my back, legs, and buttocks.

At 6 A.M., the jailers brought us cups of steaming coffee and a plate of syrup-soaked fried bread. I gave away the syrup and bread and settled for the cup of coffee as I continued to wait. Three hours later,

Deputy Jack Hill and his partner came for me. Both were surprised that I'd stayed in the drunk tank overnight and were aggravated, too, over the amount of petty paperwork they had had to complete for my one-night stand in Wichita Falls.

Once we arrived at the Medical Arts Building, we located Dr. Bibb's offices. Richard Bibb is a small, dark man with intense eyes and a mild demeanor. After a few routine quesitons, and one psychological test, we discussed my feelings about the case, and how I was dealing with its particular pressure and the recent loss of my father. Before leaving, Dr. Bibb told me, for what it was worth, that he believed I was telling the truth about having nothing to do with the abduction and murder of Johnny Turner, Jr. Actually, it meant a great deal to me, since he was the first person who believed in me outside my family and a handful of friends.

As the February sun moved out of the western sky, mingling hues of purple and gold in an azure winter sky, we drove towards Lubbock. I hadn't slept in thirty-six hours and had only eaten one meal. Once reprocessed into the jail, I immediately went to sleep.

Two days later, my attorneys and I had a long discussion about the status of the case. I was told that the State hadn't gathered any additional evidence. Their theory still rested on identifications of the so-called "witnesses." There was no physical evidence, except for a photograph of a tire print that the detective insisted my truck had made near the location of the body.

Again, Hall and McGill told me that they felt we could win the case without putting my wife, mother, or nephew on the stand. Instead, our rebuttal would be made during cross-examination. The final choice was mine, of course, and I told Mark and Dennis I needed some time to think about it. They agreed that the decision was an important one, and hard to make, and that they'd return the following Monday.

That night, I called Ma and Josie and asked them how they felt about taking the witness stand in my defense. Both were willing to testify, as was Casey. I told them I'd decide over the weekend, although I'd already made up my mind.

I felt that both women had been through enough in the past ninety days. It would be too cruel, too selfish to ask them to testify. Since my lawyers intimated that their testimony wasn't needed, I decided to spare Ma and Josie. I couldn't see them sitting there under the gaze of a crowded courtroom who had surely gathered for the thrill surrounding a murder trial. I wanted to protect them from the scathing inquisition of the district attorney, who was famous for his theatrics and merciless attacks on defense witnesses.

When Hall and McGill returned, I told them I'd go along with them, and both seemed pleased. McGill remarked before leaving, "Phil,

I think you've made a very wise decision." In less than three weeks I'd learn how wrong he was and how unwise my decision had really been. I can't say that I regret that Josie and Ma were spared, even though this meant that I would not win my case; sometimes a supreme amount of sacrifice is necessary to protect those one loves most. Still, had I known in advance that the case was already lost, my mother and both Josie and Casey would have been placed on the witness stand. At the time, however, I wholeheartedly shared what I thought was my lawyers' informed optimism.

March 1, 1978 was cold and cloudy with a strong north wind howling down the South Plains, keeping a heavy snowfall from melting. I was called from my cell and told the trial might be delayed. My attorneys didn't give me any reason. Something had come up, which I thought very strange indeed. Further, I was told to be ready for still another pretrial hearing to be held the following day when we'd seek to have additional funds granted by the bench for the private investigator. The next day, in the 140th District Court, I sat listening to Judge Shaver routinely deny each motion my attorneys presented. The motion for more investigative funds was turned down unless the investigator would tell why he needed more funds, while to do so would reveal our strategy. Finally, Judge Shaver ordered that the trial would begin as scheduled on March 6, 1978, and that I would be transferred the following morning.

The mood of the legal system seemed to change, including, most noticeably, the mood of my own court-appointed counsel. I couldn't put my finger on it, but felt that something important was being withheld from me that I needed to know. I still feel that way.

I was awake, packed, and ready to go by 5 A.M. It was a relief to see that the friendly Jack Hill would be my deputy escort to Wichita Falls, and would be assigned to guard me during the trial. The other man assigned to guard me and drive us to Wichita Falls was a Texas Ranger named Joe Hunt, who turned out to be a real gentleman.

The sun peeked above the rim of the eastern sky. It was the last dawn I've seen. We sped along the mesquite-covered country, past the 6666's ranch headquarters, and into the Red River country surrounding Wichita County while the radio blared country and western music.

When we arrived just after 9 A.M., I was processed into the population of the county jail and received a list of prospective jurors from the local attorney who'd been assigned to assist my lawyers. As we sat in the small holding cell adjacent to the booking office, the Wichita Falls attorney asked, "Why did you do it?" and then sneered when I told him I didn't do anything. His disbelief instantly eroded my confidence.

After he took his leave, I was taken to the small, steel room that would be my cell during the trial. Seven feet long and five feet wide, this chamber was lit by a twenty-five watt bulb which was enclosed in a wire mesh box in the center of the ceiling. On one wall, a small shelf and seat were welded into place, affording me a cramped writing surface. Along the other side of the room ran a metal bunk with no springs. A thin, foam rubber mattress, two blankets and a single sheet were the only bedding provided. It was very cold in this room, since the elevator shaft ran on the other side of the steel wall. Centered on the other wall was a stainless steel wash basin/toilet combination. By holding your finger over the only opening in the top of the sink, water pulsed out like a fountain when the button was pushed. A second button, when pressed, would flush the toilet.

What few possessions I had were quickly unpacked from the cardboard box I'd carried with me. I had a Bible, toothbrush, soap, deodorant, shampoo, a facecloth and towel, a few changes of socks, underwear, and tee shirts. My two suits were in the property-room along with a pair of dress shoes. I had nothing else with me. I lay down and slept for an undetermined time that afternoon. Waking quite hungry, I waited and waited for lunch to be brought around, until, attracting attention by knocking on the steel door, I learned that lunchtime had passed. I was not fed because the Wichita County deputies and jailers had "forgotten" I was there. This was the first of many times that I'd be forgotten and go without food or a daily shower.

On Monday morning, March 6, 1978, my lawyers arrived, and the process of hearing the jurors' excuses began and lasted through the morning, then continued after a recess for lunch that afternoon. We first met in a large courtroom where over two hundred people had been called as prospective jurors. Judge Shaver read a brief explanation about the *voir dire* jury selection process. [Literally translated, "voir dire" means to speak the truth. In law, it means the preliminary examination of prospective jurors where competency, interest, bias, etc., are considered. It is, however, hardly a faultless procedure. People sometimes deny their prejudice and serve on a jury anyway.]

Court was finally dismissed at 5:30 P.M. and scheduled to begin the next morning. After only one day, I was exhausted from the tension that had started with simply sitting on hard chairs, and included being the focal point of the legal process. As I picked through a cold, congealed dinner of black-eyed peas and fried spam with cornbread, I wondered what the days would be like after all the jurors were chosen and the actual trial began.

After finishing what I could from the plastic plate, I wrote a few letters to my family and friends who were anxiously waiting for some word. I felt distant from the machinations of the legal process. I sat in court, observing things I didn't understand, and having my questions answered in clipped whispers and scrawled notes. If a defendant can't comprehend what is going on around him in a court of law, then how can we expect a prospective juror to understand? The terminology used in court, and the specialized manner of speaking that many attorneys adopt when they're "on," is like a foreign language to many people. I wondered just how many good citizens, eager to do their civic duty, pretend to understand the convoluted explanations of legalese. I realized just how faulty the American system of justice might be, even though it is ostensibly the best in the world.

In my dim, solitary cell, an exhaust fan droned on through the night. The light burned, too weak to read by, and too bright to sleep with comfortably. Each time the elevator would come to the fifth floor and new prisoners were brought in, I'd wake up confused and try to go back to sleep, changing positions frequently as the hard steel beneath the thin mattress cut into my hips and shoulders.

Once when I was half asleep, I heard noises in the short hallway that ran in front of my cell. I jumped up, and through the small plexiglass window I watched in horror as a tall, thick-set Wichita County deputy repeatedly struck a black man on the head and shoulders with his night stick. The man was lying on the floor of the crowded drunk tank and the other men inside the fetid tank were cowering against its walls, shouting at the deputy to stop his assault. The black man lay still a moment, then went into what I recognized as a grand mal seizure. The deputy stepped back in surprise, then turned, and, with another officer, left the tank quickly. When they returned moments later with two of the main trustees, the four of them scooped the injured man off the floor and laid him on a filthy mattress. Then they dragged him out of the cell and out of my line of vision, but not before I saw his bruised and battered face and head.

I couldn't sleep, but smoked one cigarette after another and paced back and forth. During the night, the deputy who hit the drunk man looked in at me malevolently and said, "You didn't see anything, dead man!" Then he slammed the steel window covering and the light went out above me.

The next morning as I ate breakfast, I had a chance to ask one of the trustees what had caused the assault, and was told the man had suffered a seizure from alcohol withdrawal. When the jail guard was called to assist him, all he did was beat the prisoner. The trustee told me the black man was taken to a hospital and all charges against him were dropped, but he had looked in bad shape when he'd been hauled away.

In court that morning, I told Mark and Dennis about what I had seen the night before, and they both seemed concerned but also advised that I "not make trouble."

On the first full day in court, we heard eight prospective jurors and, surprisingly, selected the first two. On March 8, twelve prospective jurors were heard and three selected. The prosecution and defense, as well as Judge Shaver, seemed pleased that the selection was going well and I was pleased that the trial would soon begin. I looked forward to my release and rejoining my family.

The following day, we all worked very hard, hearing eighteen jurors but choosing none. Later that night in my cell, I was surprised when Mark and Dennis stopped by. They told me that one of the jurors had had a death in her immediate family. They wanted to know if I'd agree to release her from jury duty and fill her place with another juror. Of course I agreed. I knew how painful it was to lose a close relative, and not be allowed to attend the services and have the support of your family.

On March 10, we heard fifteen more prospective jurors and picked three women. Afterwards, Judge Shaver adjourned the proceedings until Monday at 8:30 A.M. I returned to my cell and answered letters until late that night, when one of the sergeants looked in, and, seeing that I was awake, asked me if I'd like to go down to Number Two Tank and play some cards with the men. I readily agreed since, after seven nights in solitary confinement, I needed human contact and diversion.

After meeting the few guys in Number Two Tank and answering their many questions about my case, we got down to some serious card playing. Most of them were younger than I, except for an old man in his seventies and another man near my age. It was enjoyable, and in the next two days, the same sergeant was on duty and generously allowed me to play cards on both nights. I spent almost eight hours out of my cramped, cold solitary cell that weekend, and so was feeling good the next morning when I went back to court.

On March 13, 1977, Deputy Jack Hill and I returned to the courtroom at 8:30 A.M. and spent a few minutes chatting, as had become our habit. When my attorneys arrived, I was told that another juror was in the midst of a family crisis. With that new wrinkle on my mind, I was only half listening to the proceedings that day as three more jurors were selected. The following day, we quickly chose the eleventh and twelfth jurors.

After several jurors had been sworn in, I stood up to go into the jury room where a small lavatory was, as had been my habit. Jack Hill was close behind me. The D.A. saw me heading for the room and jumped up and yelled for Mr. Hill to "get in there with him—there are windows in there and he might try to escape!"

Immediately, my attorneys jumped to their feet and objected to this outburst. Dennis called for a mistrial since two of the jurors who had been on the prospective juror's list, but had not yet been questioned, were still in the room during the outburst. After some verbal sparring, Judge Shaver denied the motion for a mistrial, but instructed the attorney to control himself. His behavior was totally uncalled for.

There was one window in the bathroom that was twelve inches wide and eighteen inches long. Even if I had wanted to escape, which I didn't, the courtroom was on the third floor of the Wichita County Courthouse.

Up to that time, the district attorney had barely acknowledged my presence, treating me instead with cold indifference. I'd expected some hostility from him and was puzzled by his calm demeanor. After that morning's outburst, however, I knew he was just warming up for the trial. As the time for the trial drew nearer, tension mounted in preparation for the contest of wits.

By the end of the day, the eleventh and twelfth jurors were chosen, and then sequestered in the dormitory located on the fourth floor of the courthouse just below the jail. The following day, trial didn't convene until 1 P.M. so both sides could use the morning hours for preparation. When we did convene, I was able to chat briefly with Ma and Josie, who would be watching from the gallery. Both were nervous and apprehensive about the upcoming testimony.

The purpose of the Wednesday afternoon session was to reacquaint the jury with the rules of the trial. Judge Shaver read the laws governing their duty, and the respective duties of the State and the defense. After the jury was dismissed, a "Martinez" hearing was held. [A "Martinez" hearing is where the trial judge reviews the manner in which a lineup was conducted; whether the defendant on trial was represented by counsel during the lineup, and whether the other members of the lineup were reasonably similar in appearance to that of the defendant so as not to attract undue attention to him.]

After the judge looked at the photographs of my lineup, he ruled them inadmissible and stated that showing these photographs would prejudice the jury. Other motions were filed, including a motion to quash the indictment, but these were not granted.

At 3:30 P.M., court was dismissed until 9 the following morning. As I walked out of the courthouse, I saw Jerry Robinson and Armando Ramirez standing in the hallway with the detective from Lubbock and several of his associates. I looked at Jerry, but he wouldn't meet my glance. When I looked at Armando, he shook his head slightly and gave a little shrug, then turned his back to me.

Back in the dark hole, I ate the first hot supper served since I'd come to Wichita County, and spent most of the night reading my well-worn Bible and praying. Never a Bible reader before, I found comfort in those ancient words that others had always told me about. As I read through the night, one of the most reassuring parts of the Psalms read: "My times are in thy hands . . . ." (Psalms 31:15). I knew this had to be my truth regardless of what the future might bring. I repeated that phrase that night and the next morning as I got ready for court. On that day I would be set back on the course of my life, or it would be forever altered and plunge me into the endless days and nights of prison and/or death. With these somber thoughts, I entered the courtroom just after 8 A.M., and went to talk with Josie and Ma, who sat alone, waiting. They were the only two people in the quickly-filling gallery whom I knew.

EIGHT

Our rapid-fire conversation was cut short when the district attorney entered the courtroom, followed quickly by the defense counsel. I clasped the hands of my mother and wife and smiled in a manner which I hoped was encouraging, although fear boiled inside me like hot, bitter bile.

The bailiff and the jury entered next, and then came the middle-aged court reporter, who seated herself down nervously and arranged her desk paraphernalia, only to rearrange it several more times before the judge came in and the trial began.

The first witness called the Lubbock attorney, Warren Goss. After being sworn in, the D.A. asked Mr. Goss if he knew me, establishing for the jury, I assume, that I was who they already knew me to be. Mr. Goss then told the jury that he had seen me at the intersection of 13th Street and Avenue J (which is where his office is located), but didn't elaborate or explain why. When the district attorney had no further questions, I was rather surprised. But when my own attorneys stood and told the court they had no questions, I was shocked. Mr. Goss' only other statement was to clarify the time he saw me, "between 4 and 5 P.M." Since my appointment was for 4 P.M. sharp and I'd only spent a few minutes with him, I felt that his nonchalant attitude concerning the time factor was negligent.

The second witness called was a young black, who looked around thirteen years old. Both my attorneys turned crimson, and Mark Hall hastily scribbled a note that they knew who he was but weren't expecting his testimony. We could barely hear the young man when he told the court that his name was Teddy Robinson. Answering the questions that the D.A. put to him, the witness said that on the afternoon of October 26, 1977 at approximately 5:20 P.M., he saw Johnny Turner, Jr. riding in a white pickup driven by a white, adult male with a full beard. Mr. Griffin then asked Robinson if he could identify the man he said he saw and if that man was in the courtroom.

Looking shyly towards the defense table where I sat, the youngster pointed his finger at me and said, "That's him."

During cross examination, McGill asked the Robinson boy if he'd remembered talking with him and Mark Hall, which the young boy said he recalled. McGill then asked if he recalled telling them that he didn't get a good look at the face of the man who was allegedly driving away with Johnny Turner, Jr.

Young Robinson seemed ready to cry, looked at his mother for support, and then looked at the district attorney, who sat with his eyes focused on a legal pad in front of him. McGill questioned Robinson until he admitted he hadn't seen the Turner boy get into a white pickup and described his posture as "just riding." The only thing Robinson was now positive about was that he'd seen the Turner child riding in a white pickup with a bearded white male whose face he didn't see; that he only saw his clothing well and the beard. It seemed likely to me that the youngster had been coached. The prosecutor's underhanded ploy had me seething. I *had* seen the Robinson boy before; he had been standing by a soft drink machine in the hallway, as Jack Hill and I had walked past him and into the courtroom that very morning!

I looked at the jury, but none of them seemed moved. One of the younger jurors was looking impatiently at his watch and tugging at the long hair at the nape of his neck.

I had heard plenty about the next witness from Hall and McGill. During the pretrial days at Lubbock County Jail, the three of us had talked about her as the prosecution's strongest witness. She had been the only person at the lineup who was sure about my being the man with the missing Turner child.

She was a black woman in her mid-thirties, college-educated, and a teacher in the private school that her mother had founded and operated in east Lubbock. As she climbed into her chair and settled her ample weight, a cold, calculating look passed from her eyes into mine.

Cecile Hunter testified that she saw Johnny Turner, Jr. in a pickup at a service station located at 34th Street and Quirt Avenue in Lubbock, Texas at about 5:15 on the afternoon of October 26, 1977. She said that her attention was drawn to the particular scene because the white, adult male who was also in the pickup was "poking çigarettes at the boy." She then testified that the white man got out of the pickup, walked around to look at some tires, then went inside the station to pay the attendant.

The D.A. asked Mrs. Hunter if she could identify "the white, adult male" she said she had seen and if he was in the courtroom. Without hesitation, she promptly pointed her accusing finger at me and stated, "That's him, right there, with the beard!"

Upon cross-examination, the witness modified her statement about the white male "poking cigarettes . . ." to "offering cigarettes" to the child. Furthermore, she stated that she didn't actually know the Turner child, but identified him because of a "strong resemblance to his father," whom she knew only on sight. Concluding her testimony, she maintained that the little black child and the white, bearded male drove away going south on Southeast Drive and out of her sight.

After Mrs. Hunter was dismissed, Judge Shaver called for a brief recess and I spoke with my counsel, then managed a few words with Josie and Mama. My mother seemed close to losing her self-control, and in an aside to Josie, I reminded her that if Ma should start to break down under the emotional strain, I urged her to get Ma out of the courtroom and not give the press anything sensational to write about during the trial.

As testimony resumed, the court called the owner and operator of the service station to which Hunter had referred. Mr. Davis testified that he waited on a white, adult male with a full beard driving a white pickup truck which also contained a small, black boy. Davis stated that this occured on October 26, 1977 at about 5:15 P.M.

He further stated that he didn't pay much attention to the child except to think it was odd that a black child would be riding with a white, adult male. When asked what the young boy was doing while in the service station, Mr. Davis stated that he was "just sitting in the truck." Davis finally stated that he couldn't be sure that the man sitting at the defense table was the same person he'd seen almost five months before at his service station.

I felt that this last statement redeemed him. In view of the testimony presented thus far, no one had been absolutely positive that I was the person with the black child; the only witness who was sure had said she didn't know the Turner child personally, but felt he bore a strong resemblance to Johnny Turner, Sr., whom she knew only by sight.

The next witness was an employee of the service station owner, Ray Dunn. He testified that a white pickup truck *similar* to the pickup I owned was in the service station on October 26, 1977 and that the vehicle contained two males—one black and one white. This took place, he stated, between 5:50 and 6:00 P.M.

Mr. Dunn told the court he couldn't be sure of the age of the black male and stated that "he could have been anywhere from two to twenty-two years old." Hearing this, the jurors sat up in unison and keenly looked at the witness. The D.A., sensing their reaction, pressed on but with less enthusiasm. "I would ask you whether or not this is the man, or can you tell whether or not this is the man that was in the station that day?" he asked, and Dunn replied, "Well . . . I believe it is. I, uh, couldn't positively say because, like I said, I didn't really look that close, but I believe it is."

Mr. Dunn then substantiated previous testimony that the white male was out of the truck for as long as five minutes, and that he drove away toward Southeast Drive. As for the actions of the black male, he said, "He just sat in the truck."

Judge Shaver dismissed Dunn and granted the motion from my attorney to call a noon recess. The trial would resume at 1 P.M. I talked a moment with my family and then walked with Deputy Hill to the elevators. I looked forward to quiet time alone in my cell and had no appetite for lunch.

Much to my dismay, the desk sergeant told a fellow officer to lock me in the hold-over cell that directly faced the office so they could "keep an eye on me." My plate of fried fish, potato salad, and beans was handed to me, my shoes taken, and the door locked. I picked through the food and ate only a small amount, but drank all the iced tea. Smoking was forbidden, so I spent the time I'd relished for relaxation by staring at the clock on the wall, watching the minutes pass as the second hand inched its way around the face.

An hour passed before Deputy Hill reentered the jail area. Stepping off the elevator, I lit a cigarette and walked with him back to the courtroom, where we stood talking until it was time to begin.

Up to that time, the witnesses hadn't been very damaging, nor had they been very credible. The testimony had placed me in Lubbock between 4 and 5 P.M. at Goss's office. The young black teenager had admitted that he couldn't be sure the white man he'd seen with Johnny Turner, Jr. was me, and neither could Dunn nor Davis. If Dunn was to be believed, we had to accept the statements that he identified a pickup with scratches on the side as being similar to mine, yet made no positive identification of the driver or the age of the individual next to him.

Cecile Hunter was initially assertive but weakened under cross-examination, leaving the impression, to me at least, that she wanted very badly to be sure of what she had testified, but could not be. I only prayed that the jury was paying as close attention to these points as I was.

Jerry Robinson testified next and stated, in a nervous manner quite unlike himself, that, on October 26, 1977, he and Armando Ramirez had seen me driving up behind them from the north at approximately 6:30 P.M. and that it appeared I came from the direction of Yellowhouse Canyon or "Horseshoe Bend," which is in that area. Jerry pointed me out to the court as the man he saw, which was ludicrous. My identity was well-established in the court; Jerry and I had been "friends" for months. Of course he knew me!

Armando Ramirez next took the stand and parroted Jerry's testimony in the same nervous, halting tones. Both said they had seen me from the rear-view mirror in the car; Robinson was driving, Ramirez, the passenger.

In view of their statements that I "appeared" to come from Horseshoe Bend, both admitted, under questioning by Mr. McGill, that there were several other roads I could have come from (and, in reality, did). Both stated that when seen, I was alone in the pickup, and after talking a few moments, we all drove away agreeing to meet at my house.

As they were cross-examined and then dismissed, I was angered to the point of losing my self-control that my counsel did not pursue the fact that I'd met with Jerry and Armando in the early afternoon before going to Lubbock, and agreed at that time to meet them later at my house. Also, I knew from what they'd told me at the time, and from past events in general, where to find them after work.

I still maintain that if this information had been brought out in detail, it would have explained the chain of events which the prosecutor was skillfully twisting to his own advantage. Yet, the prosecution continued to elicit only those parts of the truth that would, of course, support their allegations.

I took notes all through the trial and would write notes to both Hall and McGill suggesting questions to ask. Yet, they did nothing but barely touch upon the events in their cross-examination. It seemed that the entire mood and motivation of my counsel had changed; they no longer seemed to try.

I glanced behind me where Mama and Jo were sitting in quiet resignation, seeing my mother shake her head slowly and sadly. I knew what she meant. The trial was fast becoming a farce. I remembered what I'd read once: "It's not the truth that matters, but what people believe is the truth in a court of law."

Dr. Jose Diaz-Esquivel, a pathologist from Amarillo, Texas, was called by the State, and testified that the kidnapped boy was asphyxiated by "some manner and means used to cover the victim's mouth and nose." There was no damage done to the throat or thorax area, which, in the doctor's opinion, eliminated the possibility of actual physical strangulation. The doctor testified that there was a significantly traumatic blow to the left side of the face that was of such force that it could have rendered him unconscious, in addition to virtually separating the muscle tissue from his cheek.

Dr. Diaz-Esquivel further testified that the body sustained several shallow stab wounds on the trunk area of the body. Under further questioning, he explained that any of these wounds " . . . in and of themselves would not have been sufficient to cause death and, in fact, were more than likely caused after death." No damage was done to any of the internal organs of the deceased child. There was no evidence of any sexual involvement. There was, however, extensive maggot infestation in the various orifices of the body which, Dr. Diaz-Esquivel explained to the court, "is the purpose of the maggot: to clean up carrion wherever it is found, be it human or non-human . . . ," in cold, objective tones.

The next witness called was a chemist from the Texas Department of Public Safety, who testified that after extensive examination of my white pickup truck, he found absolutely no evidence to connect it with the deceased or to the area where the deceased was finally found.

The detective from Lubbock testified in detail about the disappearance of the child from the area of his parents' home, and the seven-day massive search by Lubbock County law enforcement personnel. With maps, charts, and diagrams, he pointed out the location of the search area and the body's location almost three miles from where they were searching. He failed to mention, however, that an anonymous phone tip to the local bondsman had told the police where to look. He only indicated that the area was off the main roads and in a steep ravine that bordered a cotton field.

The officer testified that the body was under some brush, that it was partially nude: the shirt was missing, and the pants and underpants were pulled below the knees to the ankles. The body had on tennis shoes and was identified by markings which the parents provided. He said that the body had apparently been there for an undetermined number of days. He further stated that the body was hard to find due to the rugged terrain of the area.

The district attorney picked up several photographs and handed them to the policeman, who identified them as photographs taken of the area, the location of the body, and the body itself. These articles of evidence were then passed to the defense, who examined them. Then they were entered into the court record and properly marked.

The D.A. then picked up another photograph and asked the detective if he could identify it. He stated that it was a photograph of some tire tracks that were found at the scene: ". . . In my opinion, these tracks are the same tracks that would be made by a pickup like the defendant's."

Upon cross-examination, he admitted, however, that the Lubbock Police Department had the means to take measurements of tire prints, and had the equipment available to take plaster casts of tire prints, but he could not give a definite reason why this precaution to preserve evidence had not been taken. Instead, he had relied on his " . . . own judgment as a police officer."

The most amazing inconsistency was the detective's statements that this tire print had remained undisturbed for a week in an open field, and that it had neither rained nor had the wind blown sufficiently to disturb the print. The weather on the day after the little boy's disappearance had been wet and misty with scattered showers that afternoon. And on the morning after my "All Hallows' Eve" arrest, the wind blew fiercely.

There was no mention made of the manner in which I was arrested. Nothing was said about the lie I'd been told by the Slaton sergeant, drawing me out of my house and into the snare that awaited me. No one mentioned the anonymous phone call to the police, via the bondsman's office, telling them precisely, within feet, of where the body was to be found, and that the call was made after I was arrested and held incommunicado. No one associated with the Lubbock bail bond office was called to substantiate my times of arrival and departure from their office. Neither was Warren Goss reexamined to explain why I was in Lubbock at all. The truth suffered in the courtroom—and then it died.

The final two witnesses of the trial were the most pathetic. Mr. and Mrs. Johnny Turner, Sr. were called to give their brief accounts of what had happened. Pain and stress were reflected in their faces. I couldn't bear to think of myself being in a similar situation: our children tie us to the best things in life and make us feel worthwhile. To be a parent is a great honor and a greater responsibility. Losing a child is a cruel, hurtful burden that must dim the light of life forever by its heartbreak.

Both Turner parents testified that they gave no one permission to take their child away from the Coronado Apartment area. Mrs. Turner tearfully identified her son's small tennis shoes which were recovered with the body. It took every bit of strength I had to hold back my tears. How well I could identify with them, separated as I was from my own children. Yet, I knew that even if the separation was for a long time, Stephanie and Amber would still be alive. How I ached to tell them that I was not the person responsible. But I could do nothing but sit quietly. Then I realized I was praying, my trial notes forgotten since Dr. Diaz-Esquivel's testimony.

As Mrs. Turner stepped from the witness stand and left the hushed courtroom, I looked at the jury and saw twelve sets of eyes staring back at me with thinly-veiled animosity. Only two women seemed to have a touch of pity in their expressions. Only two.

The district attorney walked across the room to the evidence table. He slowly picked up the little pair of soiled blue jeans, the tiny shoes, and the pictures of the body that I'd been loath to look at when passed to me by counsel. He placed these items of evidence in a cardboard box, and then quietly, almost reverently, asked Judge Shaver for a recess.

After a brief period of time with Ma and Josie as the deputy looked on, our shared reinforcement noticeably superficial, court was reconvened. The prosecutor summed up the day's testimony in swift, clipped tones, and his closing, "The State rests, Your Honor," was like music to my ears.

McGill rose to his full stature and simply said, "Your Honor, the defense rests," and sat down again. I felt as if I'd been hit from behind. I almost blacked out. I'd expected more than that, much more than those five words which rang in my head, hollow, empty, forboding. I turned to see how Ma and Josie were reacting and saw their pain etched deeper, as a solitary tear made its way down Josie's cheek.

The D.A. was back on his feet, asking the judge for permission to give the closing arguments the following day, since it had been a very long, full day. My counsel had no objections, so the gavel fell with court to be convened the next morning, Saint Patrick's Day.

NINE

After I was returned to my cell and ate dinner, I went to shower in Number Two Tank, but spent very little time talking to the men. They were anxious to know how the trial had gone that day, but I simply didn't know myself.

After an hour or so, I rapped on the door and asked the officer to take me back to my cell. There, the fan droned on, the hours passed slowly, and my mind continued to review the evidence which had been amassed against me.

What evidence? The people who had paraded their impressions before the court were hardly sure of what they'd seen. The young Robinson boy had changed his story. The two station attendants had been unable to state definitely it was I whom they had seen. Only the Hunter woman was adamant in her identification.

The State's chemist had found nothing. And there was nothing that the detective had said that would connect me to the scene of the crime. But the haunting thought that the jury still didn't know exactly what had happened to me kept rolling through my mind.

I dreamt that night of the flower-filled backyard of my childhood. I dreamt I was a child again, free from courts of law and death.

The small door to the cell through which our plates were passed crashed open, bringing me back to the cold, gray jail. The guard reminded me that I had only fifteen minutes to eat before he let me out for a shower. I remembered it was Saint Patrick's Day, as I emptied another plate of food into the toilet.

Once I had showered, dressed, and left the tank, the men yelled their best wishes and encouragement as I walked the long hall behind the jailer. There aren't any secrets in jail. What conversations I had had about my case were already common knowledge. Their shouts did little to bolster my hopes, but I appreciated the small show of solidarity.

Back in court, I thought how a courtroom must absorb the negative aspects of all the tragic drama that is played out there. The inexplicable feeling of dread that accompanies these places of judgment must somehow permeate the people who spend their days there. I had no time to speak to my mother and wife. The trial began, and moved swiftly as the district attorney reminded the jury and gallery of onlookers of the charges against me.

I prayed, and even as the D.A. spoke, I found myself praying for him as well. He dragged the pathetic remnants of the little boy's clothes out of the plain cardboard box, and gently laid them on the table that was parallel to the jury, then spun around and pointed his finger at me, each word of condemnation dripping with sarcastic irony.

All during the pretrial hearings, the *voir dire* proceedings, and the evidentiary proceedings, he had been for the most part, a polite, although patronizing, figure in his official duties. He now became the personification of public vengeance; the official accuser who abandoned humanity at the door to the courtroom. He would bend the laws of judgment to his personal will, supported by the power invested in him each election year and by an indulgent judge.

As I watched and listened, I saw the jury react to each word. I lost all illusions of faith in them. They were proud that they could fulfill their civic duty. The light of objectivity had long since faded. The D.A. appealed to their pride, their sense of decency, their civic-mindedness. The silence shocked us as he abruptly sat down, donning again the chameleon cloak of a humble public servant.

Dennis McGill slowly rose, and a smile passed across his pale face as he stepped lightly around the corner of the table to stand, almost shyly, in front of the jury. He asked them to consider the lack of evidence. I gripped the arms of my chair to keep myself from leaping to my feet and screaming to them that the whole trial had been a farce. I longed to dash them all with cold torrents of water, but all I could do was sit with my mask of sincerity in place, hiding from everyone but God and myself. Below the surface, though, my emotions were in riot.

Before I knew it, McGill was seated and Judge Shaver had reminded the jury of their task at hand: he advised them of the laws for a "lesser included offense" (if a jury cannot find cause to convict a defendant of capital murder, the "lesser included offense" of murder is an option they may choose). Court was adjourned as the jury filed from their seats of power into the closed chamber of deliberation.

My counsel uttered the few words they must as I waited in a small anteroom outside the courtroom. I told them I'd rather wait with my wife and mother, who stood in quiet fear outside the door. As the lawyers left, Jack Hill told my family they had to leave their purses in the hall, just in case they had smuggled weapons for me.

The scene of Ma and Josie and me remains a still photograph: a study in despair. We clung to one another and I did what I could to encourage these two strong women, forgetting for the time that I needed that too. Fifty-three minutes passed before Jack Hill stuck his head in the room and told me that the jury had reached a decision.

I entered, stood waiting for the judge, then seated myself as the jury returned and sat down. The scene, unreal yet familiar, unwound slowly as the bailiff handed the slip of paper to the judge. The verdict shattered my future, ricocheted through my mind and still reverberates. The aftershock, like those which always follow other important events, would soon follow.

I expected a repeat performance of the district attorney's *tour de force* in his closing arguments, so I was surprised how low-key his arguments were during the punishment phase of the trial. He reminded the jury of what evidence they'd heard and "justly decided on," and then sneered, "Will you allow a rattlesnake to strike twice?" Without once asking for the death sentence, he made his position clear.

McGill rose and weakly begged the jury to spare my life. Once more the jury filed out and disappeared behind locked doors.

Josie, Ma, and I waited a little more than thirty minutes before I was called back into the courtroom where the judge would sentence me to die by lethal injection, but first he thanked the jury and dismissed them, saving them from watching me stand and hear the outcome of their deliberations. Not one looked at me. I searched their faces and saw only stone masks. Yet, I wondered if they were able to go home and pretend that they had not, somehow, changed. I wondered how, after sealing my fate, they could grasp the fabric of everyday life they had briefly dropped, and not find it torn and shredded.

The gavel fell for the last time in this ordeal as the principals prepared their papers, straightened their ties, and departed with self-conscious smiles. My family and I were alone, touched by the death mandate.

Ma waited alone in the small room; with Josie close behind me and silently dying a bit inside, I entered the room and found myself unable to utter the words. All I could do was hold my arms in a pose of helpless submission and hold them both close as they held me. Our long struggle was not yet over. Indeed, it had just begun. From now on, mine would be a life without touch, without words spoken except on dreary visiting days. As we stood clinging together, Jack Hill opened the door and told me I had to go. In his hand was a set of handcuffs. His coat was unbuttoned, the butt of the .45 automatic plainly visible, a silent but clear message.

The next day, Jo and Ma came by and saw me at the jail after my first night as a condemned man. Even under the circumstances, the jailers in Wichita Falls wouldn't allow them to spend any longer than fifteen minutes, shouting through the thick, steel door as I shouted back. My attorneys had visited me the night before and had promised to reverse the decision on appeal. Except for these, they were the last people I'd see for a week.

I spent the next seventy-eight days in solitary confinement, living when I wanted simply to die and cheat the State. Each of us sometimes considers suicide. We carry the idea of self-murder around with us, as if it were a dirty little stone in the bottom of a seldom-used pocket.

I found that stone on many nights, but never took it from its hiding place. I'd never killed anyone and wouldn't kill myself. I read the Bible, and, where possible, found that it wasn't unusual for such suffering to come to those who were chosen by Christ. Chosen or not, I believed in what was written and had survived through the centuries, and it made my days and nights a little brighter.

I lived, and that was all. I existed, ate, defecated, and washed my body when the door would open and the jailers would allow me to make the now familiar trip to Number Two Tank. Most of the men I knew had since left jail; only three remained for the entire ten weeks I lived in solitary confinement in the Wichita County Jail.

I lived for the letters that came regularly to me. My mother wrote many letters, as did Josie. A few friends sent their condolences, risking emotional involvement with someone now condemned to die; someone who now felt the ultimate rejection of society. Others were unable to risk such involvement or simply didn't care. I again learned who my friends were and were not. I learned how to fill a day with reading, writing, and sleeping. Slowly, as the shock wore off, I began to look forward to each day again. The condemnation was, after all, I rationalized, just another set of words. They weren't necessarily true and need not apply, unless I accepted them and lived up to the stereotyped image they implied. Degradation was, and remains, a daily part of institutional life, but I could still control how I reacted. If the Gospel I read was true, if the Gospel was, indeed, a beacon of hope in a hopeless world, then I could claim victory in the face of defeat. Regardless of circumstances, I remained whole both in mind and spirit, as well as sound in body.

I challenged myself and God at the same time. I knew that alone I could not survive in prison, especially on death row. So, my challenge was to do as well as I could for whom I could, privately, in the name of this faceless God around which Christianity revolves. In return, this God that I was beginning to understand in my own way would give me the strength I lacked.

In that dark cell in which I froze at night and stifled during the day, I fought. I wanted to spend the remainder of my days, however long, in positive ways, so I could fight off the negative forces around me. I vowed to follow the teachings of the Sermon on the Mount, and to remember both Jesus, first, and Gandhi, second. Therein, I found a source of such strength that by the time I was told to pack up my few possessions for the trip to prison, I didn't doubt that I could accept the challenge.

We are all challenged, wherever we are. Our prisons can be like mine, made of iron and bricks. Or they can be prisons of alcohol and drugs, or bastilles of thought, trapping us within mental cells of which we are the cruelest of keepers. Knowing this, however, was but a first step to the rest of my life. I lived, as I do now, with nothing more than the idealism of peace and pacifism and the love of others to bolster me. I did not know then, and I still don't know, if this is what a Christian does or should do. In some ways, I don't care, because, after all, "Christian" is just another label. I would not preach, but practice. I would practice life, live life, and make each day count. I would take each day one at a time, which really is the only way any of us can receive them.

On May 16, 1978, I was transferred to the Diagnostic Unit of the Texas Department of Corrections in Huntsville, Texas. My old associate, Jack Hill, was one of the assigned deputies along with another deputy I knew, Sonny Keesee. It was a fast trip, with one stop for gas and another for a meal, and a few exchanges of words as the speedometer hovered around ninety miles per hour and the radio blared country and western music. Willie Nelson sang "Georgia" and "Blue Eyes Cryin' In The Rain" over and over as the Texas landscape flashed by. I longed for Texas to remain in my sight. I remember it still, a kaleidoscopic montage of spring-swelled trees and roadside flowers, whipping by my eyes, past my face and into my heart forever.

76

TEN

My escorting deputies didn't remain at the Diagnostic Unit of the Texas Department of Corrections. Jack walked over to the bench where I sat and shook my cuffed hands, wishing me luck and telling me to take care. Sonny Keesee merely waved and walked out the door. It was an hour or so later that I realized he'd failed to leave my $78.00 from the Wichita County Jail. The money could be recovered eventually, but due to this oversight, I was forced to do without any commissary privileges for the first six weeks on death row.

My impression of the Diagnostic Unit is analogous with what one might have seen in a concentration camp: lines of naked men queued up to long, makeshift tables where bored guards filled in questionnaires and pointed to the piles of relinquished personal effects. Fear was unmistakable. The stench hung in the overheated air, mingling with a camphor-like odor that drifted on the anemic breeze provided by a few fans.

I was given somewhat preferential treatment. The line of naked men was stopped and I was put in front, told to strip, then rushed past the guard who checked my toothbrush, address book, and Bible—the only things I brought with me.

After checking in, I was taken to a room where more naked individuals stood waiting, and my beard and hair were cut off, the hot clippers scratching and scorching my face. Next came a quick shower and then the delousing spray of an oily mixture that burned my eyes and genitals, so everyone left the room blinking and bowlegged.

A young guard handcuffed me and took me upstairs where I was photographed and fingerprinted. The officer in charge of the booking area seemed genuinely surprised that I hadn't been to prison before, and yet was sentenced to death row. The trustee who took the photographs wished me luck, talking quietly out of the corner of his mouth in a great impression of George Raft.

Someone who was supposed to be a doctor looked at me. That's all: he just looked. He initialed the form and stamped it with what I suppose was an "approved" stamp. I was whisked back to the new arrivals and told to stand against the wall.

I watched the new prisoners shedding their individuality, their identity, and their past, which surely they held fast in memory. I wondered if they realized, though, no matter how hard they held on to the past, they could not recapture it. They'd never be the same again. I felt it from walking into a room like this and seeing how human beings were "processed."

"Death Row!" an officer shouted. I jumped and looked at the area where the shout came from and saw a mean-looking, small man standing there glaring at me, holding a set of leg shackles and handcuffs in his left hand, a large leather belt in the other. I walked over to him and stood still, wondering if I was to be chained and publicly whipped. I was relieved, therefore, when the officer tightened the leather belt around my waist, connecting the handcuffs to it. He motioned me to follow him, and my first step sent me sprawling to the floor. At first, there was silence, then the entire room broke up in raucous laughter. I'd never worn leg irons before.

Out in the dying afternoon sun stood a van, the side door wide open, waiting for the jingling, shuffling cargo. A second officer stood nearby, his .12 gauge pump shotgun at port arms. I could not make any sudden move—like falling on my face.

The narrow bench in the back was separated by heavy gauge wire from the driver's section. While one officer careened over the side roads and past the prison fields to our destination, the other guard sat facing me, staring through my face at a dead man.

Judging from the speed and time it took to reach the infamous Ellis Unit, I figured we were almost fifteen miles from Huntsville. I was astounded at the huge building which sprawled for almost a quarter mile. I would learn later that it held 2,400 of Texas' toughest convicts. I wouldn't have been surprised to see a sign on the double gate from Dante:—"Abandon hope all ye who enter here . . . ."—but the admonition wasn't needed. Just the sight of the double chain-link fences, concertina wire, and guard towers was enough.

Within minutes, a large, rotund man walked up and signed a receipt for me, then removed my bonds. "My name is Major Steele," he said, and without waiting for a reply, turned and motioned me to follow him.

As we walked towards the prison building at a fast clip, the major told me I would do well to mind my own business, keep my mouth shut, and avoid, at all costs, the trouble that could be a part of life here. I assured him I would try.

The "mainline," as it is called, separates the kitchen and laundry areas of Ellis from the "wings" where the cellblocks are located. It is actually the spine of this elongated building, with a gym on the north end and a chapel on the south. As Steele and I walked towards death row, the last wing on the north, I watched the general population prisoners drop their eyes to the floor and walk closer to the wall. Steele, it seemed, was feared more than respected.

Each of the "wings" are given a letter and number for identification purposes. Death row was so crowded that two wings, J-21 and J-23, were used to house the condemned. I was taken to J-21 and told to strip, as the major looked through my address book and Bible. Standing there, I noticed, for the first time, the noise of caged men. Clothes were brought and I was told my cell was on the second of three tiers: Cell 2-16, so my new address was, "J-21/2-16." The major told me I had to remember that number and my prisoner identification number: Execution Number 596, or "Ex 596" for short.

I barely had a chance to see my fellow prisoners as I walked to the cell assigned me and stepped inside. I'll never forget the finality of the sound when the safety lock was snapped. I was now an anonymous unit to be fed and kept alive in my cage until execution. I was warehoused with other men with whom I shared little in common except the threat of death and the task of coping with that. The prelude to this ritualistic, revengeful death was playing itself out slowly, with unalterable determination. I felt like a crew member of a doomed ship that would not stop sinking, no matter how desperately one bailed. Life was so cheap here. I wondered how I'd manage to endure the endless hours in the five-by-nine foot cage.

The cage had been stripped clean of its former occupant's worldly goods. He left, however, blood stains on the floor, a souvenir of a stabbing. A bare mattress covered one of the two bunks attached to one wall; the rear of the cage had an open toilet and sink, both with corroded push-buttons. The sink didn't work and when I told a guard about it, he said, "So what?" and walked away.

A sixty watt light bulb barely provided illumination; beneath it was a speaker and a switch. The three-channel radio station's volume and selection were controlled by the officers at the main desk. If I listened, it would be to their taste. I wondered how anyone could hear the radio at all, so loud were the large, wall-mounted television sets that were facing the caged men.

One hears the the prison stories about obligations to other prisoners, sometimes resulting in repayment with sexual favors, so I didn't accept anything from the men who lived in the cages on either side of me. After talking with them, however, I relaxed and accepted their small loans of paper, pen, and envelopes, so I could make contact with the outside world. I wrote my mother and wife that night, and my letters were filled with self-pity and helplessness.

The months I'd spent in solitary confinement now seemed preferable to the din surrounding me. Few voices could actually be distinguished, since anyone who spoke in loud tones would be disciplined. The noise consisted of clanging doors, blaring radios, and screaming televisions. At 11 P.M., when everything was shut off, the row became silent. I sat up all night absorbing the depressing atmosphere, and assimilating as many first impressions as I could. During the early hours, a pathetic voice shattered the night with moans and screams; a man haunted by his dreams, perhaps, or by somnolent visions of times yet to come.

As the sun rose, I watched a herd of cows walking slowly to the pasture which I saw through the southern windows. As dawn became day, the line of distant trees tugged at my soul, calling, "Freedom, freedom!"

Breakfast, as with all meals here, was sloppily dropped in front of my cell; I stood waiting for someone to open the door. Finally, I realized that the army surplus tray had to be pulled under the sliding door. Later in the day, the doors slid open for a recreation period in the small, fenced pen that looked like a kennel. I walked out into the bright sunlight and stayed to myself at first, then met a few of the other death row prisoners, repeating to each one where I came from and my name. Thereafter, my days were carbon copies of despair.

The routine I'd expected and hoped for never materialized. We were fed, showered, and grudgingly allowed to walk and talk whenever the guards remembered we existed. I'd rather be hated and reviled than treated with indifference, but it was with indifference that we were treated, as if already dead. The only sure event was retribution for any minor infractions of the rules. Discipline was dispensed with calculated, practiced skill.

The first letter I sent to the prison staff was a request for a rule book. I believed there were procedures or guidelines we had to follow, but I never received a reply. One day when the administrator walked past my cell, I asked him about the book. He was taken aback momentarily, then laughed in my face and told me I'd learn about the rules as I broke them. My neighbor on death row told me later that the guards made up the rules as they went along. From what he said, we were in a classic bureaucratic inversion of Catch-22. The Texas Department of Corrections imprisoned us, barely kept us alive, and enforced an arbitrary set of petty rules on us; but because of our unique status as condemned men, we weren't entitled to the privileges that the general population prisoners were. We were, in effect, wards of our prosecuting counties, warehoused at the state prison. The only time we'd become wards of the State, in a legal sense, would be the day we were killed, or if a death sentence was commuted to life imprisonment.

Once again, I was taught the lesson of how power corrupts. From the top of the hierarchy to the bottom, the individuals who were hired, semi-trained, and charged with keeping order, actually practiced finely-honed games of emotional sabotage. By keeping the prisoners separated with a blatant racial bias, and by giving one group better treatment than the others, there could be no group solidarity. "Divide and conquer" was the working maxim, and it was magically effective. But there was another division, beyond the racial. There is a class that is kept further hidden from public scrutiny: the condemned men. We were allowed no privileges, and were, in fact, denied basic dental and medical care as well.

I simply didn't believe the stories about the unit dentist refusing to supply bridge work or dentures to the men on death row, until I experienced his particular brand of pretzel logic. Needing a temporary cap on a broken incisor, I was told I couldn't have it because, "You're on death row, boy, an' you don't need good lookin' teeth to die . . . ." He did, however, offer to pull the tooth. I declined the service.

A similar excuse was given when my request for reading glasses was denied. With the assistance of my attorney, however, I was able to have a pair of glasses made for me, nine months after the request date, and only after legal action was suggested to remedy the problem. During that summer and autumn, I expected my appellate brief to be filed, but learned otherwise. It took many months for this to happen; in some other cases, it even took years.

Once sentenced to death, one begins endless months of waiting for the trial transcript to be typed and certified by the District Court before the process of an appellate brief can even begin. More months pass until the attorneys can prepare the defendant's arguments and submit them to the Court of Criminal Appeals. Then even more time is spent while the State answers the defendant's brief. Finally, the oral arguments are presented to the court, and the waiting continues until the court can reach a decision which will either reverse the sentence, resulting in a new trial or a commuted sentence, or affirm the sentence. The latter usually results in federal appeals and petitions to the Supreme Court. In short, a man convicted of a capital offense can expect to be caged, waiting for and thinking about his death, for as short as two years and as long as ten or fifteen or more. In fact, Caryl Chessman waited for twelve years on California's death row before losing his bid for life imprisonment. In more recent memory, Gary Gilmore and Jesse Bishop spurned the long, agonizingly slow process of appeal, and voluntarily allowed their lives to be claimed by capital punishment.

What killer would hold his victim in suspended animation for months or years, constantly threatening to act but not acting? Death row, then, remains a paradoxical journey into the extreme. Optimism reigns within one man, while pessimism deafens the ears of his neighbors, making it nearly impossible to maintain any hope.

Justice William Brennan of the United States Supreme Court has said, in reference to the death penalty, " . . . . No other punishment is comparable to death in terms of physical and mental suffering. Although our information is not conclusive, it appears that there is no method available that guarantees an immediate and painless death. In addition, we know that the mental pain is an inseparable part of our practice of punishing criminals by death, for the prospect of impending executions exacts a frightful toll during the inevitable long wait between the imposition of the sentence and the actual infliction of death." It is understandable, then, that "the wait" literally becomes "the weight" on death row.

The only relief came when I'd receive visitors. Josie and Ma came first, when Jo moved to Houston to work and live with Nell, and to seek respite from the small-town prejudice of Slaton, now increased after I was sentenced to die. Through the summer and fall, she came as often as finances allowed, but when she lost her job, she was eventually unable to drive the 135 miles to see me as often as we liked. I tried to talk around the subject of capital punishment and prison, but each time our conversation would be pulled into the tragedy that separated us. Every visit ended in tears.

When my family came to see me, I would always be asked how my conditions were. The news media were increasing their coverage of a suit against the Texas Department of Corrections by the prisoners, who would be represented by the Federal Justice Department.

So, I had a choice of either fabricating stories or telling them the truth, that death row wasn't a place where men actually die, but wait for death. We die slowly, by degrees, day after day, from inside ourselves. Finally, all that remains are the shadows of our former selves, in a pantomime of life, human husks. I explained that, eventually, even a life sentence begins to have a sort of backhanded attraction in comparison with death row. I watched my family as I told them the truth. How much more thoughtful a lie would have been.

When the visits were cut short by disinterested guards, I'd walk back to death row, flowing past the hundreds of men in the general population who crowded the hallway. Their stares and open curiosity troubled me at first, but gradually I became used to it, like so many other things that were alien to me.

Many prison hours, especially on death row, are spent in contemplating the past. Each man can retreat to softer, less threatening times, and somehow erect a mental barrier against the empty tragedy of incarceration. It doesn't really matter what an individual's past has been, but rather what he believes it has been and how he projects that image to himself and to others. We each listen, waiting our turn to recall, relish, and embroider our pre-incarceration selves.

Sadly enough, a large percentage of the people on death row are so young and their pasts are so near childhood, that it is hard for them to accept their experiences as adults. Nevertheless, each man is reduced to and equalized in a similar pattern. Row upon row, stacked ceiling high, we are each victims of our own actions, victims of self-fulfilling prophecies passed on from parents, teachers, siblings, peers, and society. If a human being has failed all his life, is it any wonder that prison is his final destination? It is not surprising to listen to one young man's history, as I did, and hear his private pain at being placed in one state institution after another from the time he was eight years old, until, at the age of seventeen, he committed a robbery-murder. All society could do was place the final stamp of rejection on his bulging case history by sentencing him to death.

There is no attempt to rehabilitate, only to destroy; no attempt to understand and reconcile, only to condemn. It makes sense, then, for a man to stand as tall as he can, and hold up any shred of the past for recognition. He wants to *be* somebody, a person instead of a number. Most of my fellow prisoners and friends do not understand that we cannot regain what has been, particularly when what has been never was.

That devastating realization brings an enduring pain. You can only reconcile yourself to observe and try to understand. You may no longer select, manage, or change anything, but only stand and observe, stand and endure the consequences of being who you are and how you were shaped by the unwise and uncaring entities who touched you.

I eventually acquired a typewriter from the prison commissary, and created a safety buffer against the boredom and despair by devising my own routine. I rose early, followed a pattern of quiet reflection and prayer, meditation and physical exercise with yoga. Then I'd write in the mornings, read in the afternoons, or assist some of the other men with their letters or legal typing. I preserved by sanity and gradually made contact with my dormant creativity. My poems were published in the prison paper, then recognition began to spread outward like ripples in the vast sea where I once had floundered alone.

ELEVEN

During October, 1978, as a show of support and solidarity for the *Ruiz v. Estelle* suit, a general inmate strike was called and swept through several units. Although we could do nothing but cheer from the sidelines, a few of us joined in the nonviolent protest by refusing to eat or shower. The fast lasted three days. Through widespread media coverage and the way in which the prison authorities overreacted, the public became aware of the sorry conditions in "the best prison system in America." I hoped that everyone had learned that our nonviolent actions were more effective than the individual, self-consuming acts of violence.

In November, I marked my first full year behind bars. Thanksgiving was upon us, and I saw Josie and Nell for the last time that year, although none of us knew that. Their unexpected visit was a joyful event that turned sad when, the next day, the warden wouldn't allow my children, my ex-wife Susan, and her husband to visit me. Death row prisoners weren't allowed visits on holidays. Susan told me that our little girls cried all the way home to Dallas, victims of a calloused old man who readily attached to them the stigma of their father's imprisonment.

The year would end with loss, as it had begun. My Grandmother Davidson would die in the Slaton Nursing Home of terminal cancer, leaving my mother with yet more grief and pain.

In mid-December, my former neighbors, J. W. and Helen Dunn, came to visit me. We sat like strangers for an hour, then tried to fill in the second hour with words that would comfort one another and bolster our sagging spirits.

Christmas arrived, heralded by apples, oranges, and traditional foods. The guards didn't allow us to shower that day, since it was a holiday and they resented having to work and be away from their families. Every man must have been thinking of home and must have felt the same sharp pangs of loneliness and abandonment. Some of us ignored our sadness and joked around the despair; others exchanged small gifts of candy or cigarettes with special friends. A few of us lay in the dark recesses of our cells and shed silent tears that were at once so familiar but never discussed.

Just after 10:30 that night, we heard two gunshots, and, for an instant, we saw three figures making a mad dash for the tall, wire fences in our field of vision. Immediately after the shots, the siren went off and the huge searchlight started its path on the windows and sides of the building. Death row exploded in cheers and shouts of encouragement to those prisoners who had managed to get out of the building from wherever they were housed in the general population.

Within minutes, the outside perimeter of the prison grounds was surrounded by cars and pickups driven by off-duty guards who lived just down the road in state houses. We could see the guards roaming around, each armed with a handgun or carbine. We saw two prisoners in postures of surrender, hands above their heads. They'd only made it over the first fence. The third prisoner was later caught nearby and marched, naked and bleeding from the wounds he had received from his captors, past the guard tower and out of our line of sight. The Texas tradition of not allowing any escapes was intact.

The week dragged on, and 1979 arrived with little fanfare. My nerves were becoming so frayed that I requested to see the unit psychologist. A week later, after we'd talked briefly, I was given a prescription for Sinequan. Its side effects were worse than those I'd been attempting to relieve. It sapped my strength so badly that I had no motivation, not even to get up in the mornings. So, after a few numb days, I told the medical officer to discontinue the medication.

My faith remained strong but tested by the stress of being locked up like a caged animal, and by the increasing lack of contact with Josie. She wrote less and less and said very little when she did. I would torture myself with the fear that so many married people have in prison: Will my spouse remain faithful to me? The odds were against it, according to the older convicts. I didn't fear losing Jo to another person, but to her own depression and escape into drinking. I had feared that her move to Houston wasn't in anyone's best interest, and now it appeared that I was right.

Jo worked with my sister, and their jobs were governed by the weather, since they worked at Houston's large construction sites. When it rained, no one could work, and 1979 seemed to be one of the wettest winters anyone could remember in a long time. As with everything that had happened in the past, I had to rely on the belief that it would work out for the best, with God's help. This active quest for the positive (and not the medication) eventually restored my health.

The first time I was able to leave the prison was when my request for eyeglasses came through. After receiving the eye exam at Ellis Unit,

I was taken to the old Walls Unit, the original prison site of the Texas Department of Corrections. The trip off the prison farm and the short drive into town was a welcome break in routine. Even the careless treatment I received by the guards was worth the drive. While they drank coffee with their friends at the Walls, I stood in the pouring rain without a jacket or hat.

Once inside the old hospital building, their behavior was like that of the old silent film characters, the Keystone Kops. Walking at double their normal speed with me shuffling along in my rattling chains, they'd shout, "Make a hole, make a hole, dead man comin' through!"

The conditioned reaction to the prisoners standing in lines and waiting for medical attention was to scurry from my path and huddle against the wall, wide-eyed, confused, and frightened. I felt like growling at them or perhaps gnashing my teeth for effect, but I contained my sarcasm.

After this experience, I thought of getting together with my fellow death row prisoners and writing how we felt about life there, and how, except for our legal differences, we were no different from other incarcerated men. The idea was, at first, accepted readily, but as days went by and the outline of the project was completed, enthusiasm waned. Some of the men even feared retribution from the authorities if we wrote anything critical about the prison. A few, however, did set down their opinions, and after editing and typing, I mailed the article to the editor of the prison paper, the *Echo*.

It never reached him. Someone in the mailroom intercepted it and we never heard about it again. I'd retained a copy, so I mailed it to him a second time. This time it was delivered without being confiscated, but was never printed.

In February, my brief for appeal was filed in the Court of Criminal Appeals, and I was notified by my attorneys that they expected to argue the case before the court later in the year. I was relieved when I received a copy of the brief, and did my own legal research into the points of error. There were at least two points that could result in a reversal, I felt. First, the indictment was faulty and should have never withstood scrutiny of the District Court Judge; secondly, the jury had answered affirmatively to questions concerning our prior criminal records, acts of violence, and psychiatric testimony, thereby branding me as a continuing threat to society. No supporting evidence for this was ever presented to the jury, because it simply did not exist. I was under the sentence of death, then, unconstitutionally. The jury had sentenced me to die, perhaps, because they had thought they were expected to.

In early May, Jo and Nell returned. Jo had little to say to me, but reading her silence, I felt it was better not to press the matter and simply remain as supportive as I could, even though I desperately needed her support in return. Her physical appearance indicated how much and how frequently she had been drinking. I knew then that it would be up to me to convince her to leave Houston. I just didn't know at the time where she might go or how I might convince her to do so.

A week later, my mother, children, and Susan arrived for our allotted time together. We held on to one another with our eyes, saying as much as we could in the limited time. My children had grown considerably and my heart ached just to touch them. Too soon, they left me to the solitary life of prison, but each letter somehow strengthened me. I was able to survive in an empty, emotionally-draining wasteland through the growing numbers of people "out there" who wrote me of their support and their love.

Since we are denied the touch of those we love, a letter or a visit is the sole thread of human contact that remains when all other ties are severed. It is infuriating to hear the excuses one sometimes gets from people who don't write. How hard it is for the prisoner to understand a loved one "not having the time" to write. Equally, how hard it must be for those in "free society" to understand the importance of steady, reliable contact through frequent letters and visits.

Our keepers know this: our weakness and dependency is used as leverage against us. The threat of losing visiting privileges is very effective, the illegal sabotage of mail similarly demoralizing.

As spring made its bright green entry into our grim and dreary world, every man on death row was given a brief embrace of new hope when the Fifth Circuit Court of Criminal Appeals reversed the death sentence of James Paul Burns and ordered a new trial. The news came on Good Friday. As the death of Jesus Christ had promised eternal life and victory over our own deaths, so did this reversal give renewed hope for some of us. Burns would have been one of the first men executed in Texas in many years. Perhaps his case and the court's ruling would help others.

Now, the political aspirants who use public fear of crime and the societal urge for revenge would have to move cautiously. It was common knowledge that the State of Texas would appeal the Fifth Circuit's decision. Should it be upheld, the State would be obliged to retry many of the men on death row or commute their sentences to life imprisonment.

The common picture that is painted of a man or woman convicted of a capital crime is that of a relentless, cold-blooded killer, a monster, an animal, an incurable psychopath who will kill and kill again. This picture defies reality. The people on death row are human beings, too. To say that they have no regard for human life and do not regret their actions is to generalize unfairly. I realize this statement simplifies a complex set of psychological and political reactions. But this is important to say: they have consciences, too. Certainly, there are those rare individuals who have no moral sense or regrets, but I myself never met a single individual on death row who fit the description that the prosecutors, news media, and law enforcement community has depicted.

The times in which we live are indeed perilous. It is not the rise of crime or inflation or the threat of war with the Soviet Union that we should fear so dreadfully. We should fear the duplicity of our moral and ethical values. It is the duplicity of unequal justice that should strike fear into the hearts of people. They should fear instead the unprincipled ambition and power of their elected officials. The roots of injustice are not to be found so much on death row or in any other prison; we should look instead to the courthouse, the district attorney's office, or even the police department. Look into the eyes of the poor, who make up the majority of our prisoners. There you will see fear—and a system which serves a privileged minority in the name of a silent majority.

TWELVE

Many times, an accused person is tried and convicted in the daily press, long before the actual trial begins. I never talked to the news media or gave interviews until mid-May of 1979, when a journalist from New York interviewed me. Mike Jendrzejczyk of *Fellowship Magazine* had been corresponding with me regularly; in the course of our letters, in which we discussed the death penalty, Mike suggested that I give Doug Magee an interview. On the first anniversary of my arrival on death row, Doug and I talked for two hours and then held a short photo session in the dayroom on death row. My statements and the poem, "Midwatch," which I had written earlier in the year, appeared in the Summer, 1979 issue of *The Journal of Current Social Issues*, my first instance of "positive press."

Doug and I also discussed John Spenkelink's impending execution in Florida. Nine days later, the State of Florida electrocuted John in the first nonvoluntary execution of the decade. As the news of John's death spread, the men on death row in Texas became quiet and reflective, thinking, as was I, perhaps, of the similar fate that might await us.

The summer of 1979 was far cooler than my first sweltering months in Ellis Unit. My time was filled with writing, and the days passed quickly. Writing, it seemed, was the only effective way I could reach out from the depths of prison and let others know what I saw, heard, and felt, and what changes I thought needed to be made. My rejection slips grew in number, but every now and then an editor would take the time to attach a note saying, "Keep trying!"

Although I was finally adjusting to prison, Josie wasn't adjusting to her own particular sentence of loneliness. Her letters were even more infrequent, and in the struggle to survive in fast-paced Houston, she found herself further and further behind in debts and other responsibilities. My mother-in-law, Janet Stewart, and I kept in close contact and prayed for Jo's problems to work themselves out, but we were both concerned. For her own sake, I manipulated Josie. Through a private agreement with her mother, Janet agreed to fly to Texas from Alaska and take Josie back with her. Jo and I had planned to go to Alaska anyway, so I felt that the new beginning for Josie would simply be spent without me.

Although there was an inevitable bit of resentment at first, Jo has since found Alaska to be home, and her previous problems no longer plague her. She was, once again, in a secure and loving environment that made the comfort of alcohol unnecessary. Needless to say, *her* relief was *my* relief, and the sacrifice of no longer seeing her was a small price to pay for peace of mind. When asked later how I could send her away, I told a friend on death row that I loved her enough to tell her goodbye—so I did.

Recreation on death row had improved somewhat from the "catch-as-catch-can" process of my early days. The new building major, A. J. Murdock, saw that we were allowed out in the sunlight at least twice a week, where we would play volleyball with wild abandon. Several of the men who lived on the first tier constructed bird nests out of empty tobacco cans and anxiously awaited hatching time. There was nearly a small-scale riot when some of the guards tore the bird houses down.

Later in the summer, one of the men I'd first met began experiencing severe emotional problems which resulted in a suicide attempt. I'd never witnessed the kind of indifference he suffered. The authorities were aware of his cries for help, yet, callous beyond comprehension, they ignored him until he slashed his wrists with a razor blade. Finally, a goon squad of guards rushed him and held him down while a medical officer sutured his wrists. A large dose of thorazine was administered and he was left alone again.

Later, in desperation, the man began beating his head against the steel bars and the sharp edges of the metal bunk. No one came to help him or restrain him until he lost consciousness. Afterwards, we learned that he'd ripped the sutures from his wrists with his teeth. He was removed from death row for a little over a week, then returned, bandaged and drugged, and once again locked in. The Catch-22 of condemnation was at work: the state hospital, while recognizing his desperate need for treatment, could not admit him, they said, because he was sentenced to die, and they didn't have the appropriate security precautions.

In his final act of anguish, he somehow obtained a glass jar which he shattered and with which he slashed his throat. Weeks passed until we heard that he had somehow survived and was being kept temporarily in the prison's treatment center. One day, however, he was returned to death row and caged again. This time, he'd been placed in a straight jacket that was left open at the back to secure him to a bare mattress on the bunk. In addition, handcuffs were placed on his wrists. A crash helmet much like a motorcyclist would wear, was placed on his head, and there he lay for weeks, helpless, alone, and drugged. The care and feeding he received was from the inmate porters. At times, he'd call for assistance for over an hour before a guard would open the door and untie him so he could urinate.

Some of the men around death row were so uncomfortable that they would mock his yelling. This was not from cruelty, but rather from an inability to deal with their feelings. He reminded us all that the gray-clad spectre of death was not the only fear we faced; the possibility of insanity also lurked in the wings.

Repressed fear and rage run so deep at times that the reaction to abnormal stress can spill out in torrents of action that, while harsh, are not surprising. The pressure cooker of life on death row exploded one morning, leaving a fellow inmate dying on the floor of his filthy cell.

One night, two men who lived next to one another had an argument and the older man threatened the younger one. When the doors to the cells were cranked open the next morning for recreation, a flurry of arms blurred momentarily; minutes later, Edward King was dragged from our midst. He was pronounced dead before the proper medical treatment could be obtained. He had sustained a single stab wound to the heart. Three days after watching his body being carried away, I acknowledged my thirtieth birthday, wondering how many more men I'd see experience a similar fate.

If only workshops in nonviolence would be provided here! If classes in effective communication could be held, how much violence might be avoided? The authorities don't provide the means by which a man can learn alternate ways of interaction, so life behind the double cyclone fences remains filled with fear and distrust.

Each of us represents the principle of life, no matter our color, shape or condition. Those behind the walls of prison are just as much a part of the human family as the Pope or President. Agreed, individuals must be held responsible for their actions, and I do not advocate the violation of law and order, or the elimination of proper checks and balances. Nor would most inmates. However, order can never be preserved so long as America supports a system of methodical, dehumanizing institutions that are nothing but a collection of cruel cages.

The simplistic attitude toward punishment that the lock-em-up evangelists of law and order (at any human cost) preach is an anachronistic stance that must be revised and altered before significant progress in real rehabilitation can begin, before emotional and spiritual healing can even start. One wouldn't expect the spontaneous remission of disease in a hospital where the staff did nothing. The same is true in other institutions. The problem of crime and criminals involves whole personalities. The dismal history of failure in providing more than indifferent custodianship to other human beings indicates the crying need for a human and humane change in our prisons. This systematic failure is not a legacy I want my children or their children to inherit. Aren't we intelligent enough to see that locking men and women in cages only results in additional misery and despair?

September and October passed, and football games became the chief source of joy and entertainment, although they disturbed my writing. I don't watch or enjoy football, so I requested and received earplugs to stop the noise, and continued to write. November arrived with cold rains, and the aches of living in damp, cave-like dwellings. On the days when it was too cold to use my typewriter, I read Gandhi, Merton, and Bonhoeffer. My life was further enriched and uplifted while life around me remained an ordeal for so many others.

I was pleased to receive notification that my poem, "Midwatch," had been selected for second prize in the Rocky Mountain Poetry Society's annual Joyce Kilmer Award. In December, an article I'd written about life on death row that had been rejected by several commercial magazines was accepted and published in *Fellowship*. The responses I received from the article brought even more contact and encouragement from outside the walls of Ellis Unit. I realized then that I would never again sink to the depths of despair that I'd known only a year before. In my active days of anti-war protesting, I had admired the Berrigan brothers very much, especially for their courage in the face of imprisonment. I was especially elated, therefore, when the first letter from Father Daniel Berrigan, S.J., arrived. We encouraged one another, he in his struggle against the madness of the nuclear arms race, and I in my personal struggle against the death penalty. Dan reminded me that " . . . we're all on death row," the truth of which rang clear and pure, and awakened me like a cold shower. We all face execution, atomization in seconds, every moment of our lives.

Christmas was blessed in 1979, and I didn't feel any revulsion at the commercialization of a capitalistic Christmas, as I had for years. Now that I knew Jesus Christ, I could celebrate the event of his birth in my cell, and was reminded that Jesus Christ had also briefly lived as a condemned man, that he died a convicted criminal. The realization was sobering. This Christmas there were no escape attempts. I prayed a simple prayer of thanksgiving for the day, and of acceptance and service for however many days I would have left to me in this life.

If I could live for each day and strive to discover the goodness in life, whether it was a smile or a warm thought or simply a day without added pain, then time would take care of itself and would be well spent. If I would have to die, then perhaps in living as well as I possibly could, I'd be able to die with respect. Life has to have meaning, and that meaning comes from within a person. I could live well and die nobly.

Just after the first of the new year (1980), I completed a volume of poetry I'd been struggling with for almost two years. Then a letter arrived that would make the writing of this book possible. I signed the contract and began the first tentative pages of the manuscript. Within weeks, I received more welcome, yet unexpected, news.

My sister and Casey visited me on Lincoln's birthday, and while we caught up on family news, Casey asked me if I had any idea when the Court of Criminal Appeals would rule on my case. I reminded him and Nell that there was no way to second-guess the court, then said, ". . . We'll probably be surprised by irony again. Remember, I was arrested on Halloween and then sentenced on Saint Patrick's Day. I expect their ruling to be on or near a holiday for some reason," and we all laughed.

At the time, I hadn't thought much about it; it was just an offhand statement to lighten the mood. The next afternoon, as I lay on my bunk reading a volume of translated Vietnamese poetry, the 5 P.M. news-caster said that my case had been reversed, and that the court had ordered I not be retried for capital murder.

I thought I was hearing things and jumped to my feet, just as voices in the other cells began to repeat the news. Knowing no other way to express what I felt at the time, I dropped to my knees in thanksgiving and prayed through a cacophony of emotions. The victory was now on my side.

I spent the remainder of the afternoon and night writing short, joyous letters to family and friends. Our prayers had been answered and life would have my heartbeat. The weight was lifted, although the wait would continue on a different level. I would have to wait for the inevit-able State's motion for a rehearing, and then for reindictment and retrial. More months than I care to count stretch before me, as I write these words and listen to the now-familiar sounds of death row. I'm no longer condemned, though, and am separated from the whole. My complete joy lasted only as long as the time it took for me to realize that so many of the men around me would never feel what I do now.

I've experienced a sort of "survivor's guilt," a feeling of joy, mingled with sadness. It was as if I'd spent years battling the raging seas with a valiant crew, and while I reached the shore, I did so knowing many of my shipmates would sing below the surface of the deep, dark water.

For this reason, I feel that I have no choice but to work against murder by mandate. Like the time, ten years before, when I was touched by the brutality of war and directed my energy against it, so now must I honor this commitment.

During my twenty-five month ordeal on death row, my faith forbade me to accept defeat. I never let go of the thought of life, never dropped the inner vision of rejoining my family, and taking up a normal, yet forever altered, life. As long as a person is able to sing the song of life, there is hope. There is happiness in that song, no matter where one may be. We must never stop believing this; we must never fail to hum the tune.

All of us, on our walk through life, stub our toes and stumble on untrodden paths; yet the walk is still worthwhile. But regardless of how poorly another person lives, even on the periphery of life, neither society nor any individual has the right to take his life or threaten to do so. This is true in the individual case, as well as in the case of one nation against another. Life is a gift beyond value. We are only caretakers: we do not own our lives, but are entrusted with them from God, and, in a great sense, we touch something holy and close to our Creator in our every breath.

On death row, a person becomes a voyeur of life. He becomes not the sum of his actions, but the sum and result of his reactions to the world in which he has walked and from which he has been banished as unfit to live. Under this prolonged, suspended life, an individual can only reflect on whatever stimuli the world projects to him. I struggled against the negative messages by immersing myself in as many positive things as I could.

From the men that make up death row in Texas, I've learned: "If you walk towards the Light, the shadows fall behind you." Knowing this, however, doesn't change the ugly fact that the dehumanization of men and women behind prison walls continues unabated. Every day, another person is brought closer to death at one end of the imprisonment spectrum, while at the other end, young, first-time offenders enter the gates and within hours become emotionally old forever.

Those who advocate murder by mandate believe that such actions deter capital crimes more effectively than the threat of imprisonment. This remains, however, both unproven and unprovable. Society appears to ignore the reality, that there is no humane way to kill someone, whether it's for the good of society or just from revenge. There can't possibly be any "good" gained by an act that devalues life.

I know that in any human endeavor, mistakes will occur. It's in this sense of understanding and tolerance that I've chosen not to level any unfounded accusations towards any of the individuals responsible for my arrest and conviction. However, I can be skeptical. There will always be those who choose to believe the worst about a person, just as there are those who would rather believe the best. Everything that happens to us can be said to be worthwhile because we can choose to learn from both the pleasant and unpleasant. The secret is to move on and not spend years repeating those experiences.

This story began while I was under sentence of death; my only wish is to set the record straight and leave behind an explanation for my children, so that, when they're old enough, they might have some answers to their questions. A kind of epitaph, one might say. Through a series of mistakes, deliberate or accidental, made in the investigation and prosecution of my case, I could easily have become another statistic added to those poor souls who've walked this way before me, and who were denied their lives because of the errors of others. If for no other reasons but the irreversibility of capital punishment and the inevitability of human error, I feel we must lay this barbarous practice aside.

Our Judeo-Christian tradition proclaims that capital punishment is a cold, calculated practice which serves no purpose and undermines an already divided and battered society. The State cannot wrap itself in a cloak of pseudo-respectability and pretend not to be a surrogate lynch mob. No amount of posturing or pretending will change the fact that killing is wrong, and that something is inherently lacking in a society which condones it. By permitting it to continue, we are all diminished. Society has the power to see that correction actually takes place by trying to help unfortunates change their lives. Imaginative dedication can provide alternatives to locking people away for terms of desperation, decay, and death.

One might argue that we are not our brother's keeper. We are, however, responsible for how we live, as individuals and as a civilized society. No amount of law enforcement, punishment, teaching, or preaching will demonstrate this to others as effectively as refusing to kill those who have been found guilty of killing others. We must set our own example.

Perhaps that's what the prophet Ezekiel meant when he wrote: "As I live, says the Lord God, I have no desire for the death of the wicked. I would rather that a wicked man should mend his ways and live" (Ezekiel 33:11).

www.ingramcontent.com/pod-product-compliance
Lightning Source LLC
Chambersburg PA
CBHW031522270326
41930CB00006B/489